MW01485048

# My Box of
# Chocolates

# My Box of Chocolates

How my child with autism learned to read, write and more

**A Memoir**

GORETTI E. RERRI

This is a non-fiction work. Names and characters other than those of the author's family have been changed to protect the privacy of the individuals. Places mentioned are real.

My Box of Chocolates: How My Child with Autism Learned to Read, Write and More

Published in the United States of America by Goretti E. Rerri

Copyright © 2018 by Goretti E. Rerri

All rights reserved

Editing by Kyle Cushman of Word Artisan VT

Editing by Dr. Christine B. Uduebo, of Kritik Associates, NY

This book is protected under the copyright laws of the United States of America. Any reproduction or other unauthorized use of the material or images herein is prohibited without the express written permission of the author.

First Printing:        First Edition:
Rerri, Goretti

My Box of Chocolates: How My Child with Autism Learned to Read, Write and More
Website: www.myboxofchocolatesbygrerri.com

This book is available for purchase on Amazon.com and other major distribution channels.

ISBN: 0692973087        ISBN 13: 9780692973080
Library of Congress Control Number: 2017910457
CreateSpace Independent Publishing Platform
North Charleston, South Carolina

# Book Review

"So many things that we take for granted like dressing, bathing, counting and shopping for groceries are in fact complicated social interactions that we perform without thinking. However, these are not trivial to teach, especially to someone with autism who processes information differently. In that sense, this book is especially eye-opening, both in terms of how hard it must be to navigate the modern world with conditions like autism as well as to how complex many supposedly simple activities are.

Another remarkable thing about the book is how engaging it is. We see the world through the eyes of both Teresa as well as Goretti Rerri. We are able to feel their struggles and celebrate their victories…Reading this book is thus extremely easy and pleasurable.

The willingness of the author to talk about the difficult moments… makes the book that much more engaging. We are truly able to relate to the characters in the narrative.

This book is rated 4 out of 4 stars."

*-OnlineBookClub.org*

# Dedications

*This book is dedicated to all parents and guardians caring for children and adults with developmental and intellectual disabilities.*

**In Memory**
To the memory of my loving mother, Mary Senera Rerri

# Acknowledgments

I wish to thank the doctors, teachers, teacher aides, therapists, and other professionals and service providers through the years who have worked and continue to work with my daughter, Teresa. Their efforts have yielded great results. I thank Kyle Cushman of Word Artisan VT for her fresh perspective in revising and editing the manuscript. My gratitude goes to my niece, Dr. Christine B. Uduebo, of Kritik Associates NY, whose "eagle eyes" for details and suggestions were invaluable.

My appreciation goes to Dr. Bisi Gwamna, my longtime friend, for believing in me and encouraging me along the way. I'd also like to thank my incredible friend, Polly Shupe, for painstakingly, proofreading my manuscript, and, making valuable suggestions for improvement.

I am indebted to my daughter, Elohor, who provided support, talked things over, offered candid opinions, and assisted in the editing and proofreading of the manuscript. My gratitude goes to my son, Ovie, for his encouragement and support.

Last, but not the least, I thank my precious daughter, Teresa, through whom I discovered my life's purpose.

# Table of Contents

# Introduction

In the movie *Forrest Gump,* one of Forrest's most famous lines is: "My mama always said, life was like a box of chocolates. You never know what you're gonna get." That is so true! Like every other parent, I expected that my baby would grow up to be a typical child and everything would be just fine. However, things did not turn out as I presumed.

Teresa was diagnosed with autism spectrum disorder (ASD) just before her fourth birthday, and the behaviors associated with ASD that she exhibited were very different from those of typical kids. Consequently, educating and raising her was a far cry from what I had envisioned. Since her diagnosis, our ride through life has been anything but ordinary. It has been and still is a peculiar adventure.

*My Box of Chocolates* tells about the struggles and successes surrounding my daughter's education starting from birth to high school graduation.

The extraordinary nature of our journey prompted me to write about it, and I hope that our story will help to increase awareness about the condition of autism and the unique challenges it presents. I wish that the book will positively influence the way others look at people with autism in spite of the symptoms they present. Most importantly, I hope that our experiences will inform, empower, and inspire parents of young children with autism.

The names of all of the characters in the book except those of my family have been changed.

The term *autism spectrum disorder* (ASD) will be used interchangeably with the term *autism* throughout the book.

# One

### Diagnosis

## New York City
## 1992

I t was barely nine in the morning when the phone rang one hot summer day at our apartment in New York City.

"Mrs. Zoma, this is Angie from the office of special education in Queens," a woman said, her tone serious and professional. "We would like to invite you to come down to the office because the psychological evaluation results for your daughter are ready, and we need to share them with you in person."

*Why would they need to tell me in person?* I thought. *This does not look good.* "Okay. On my way." I replied.

I dressed Teresa as quickly as I could, feeling a low-grade anticipatory adrenaline flow as I did so. Luckily she was cooperative. I quickly pulled her hair back into a ponytail. Tall for her age, and skinny in her orange leggings, white tee shirt, and little white sandals, she looked beautiful, despite my hurried approach to dressing her for the day.

I then hailed a cab by the curb, and we started off to the office. Slumped by my side, Teresa turned to look through the window at the city rushing by. When a faint ray of sun fell on her face, she fended it off with cupped hands and spontaneously blurted out meaningless id-iosyncratic gibberish, something she usually did when she felt excited about something. Although she was 4 years old, she was still virtually non-verbal and communicated mostly by pointing, grabbing, or taking my hand and walking me to her object of interest. She was usually hyper-active, but during this ride, she sat quietly for the most part.

As I sat in the yellow cab beside her lost in thought, I stared out the window at the passing shops and pedestrians without really seeing them. *Why is this evaluation different? Why do they need to see us in person?* The results of four other evaluations—speech, socio-emotional, physical, and motor skills—were shared through written reports that were mailed to me.

I did not even notice we had reached the office of special education until the cab driver broke into my thoughts.

"Ma'am, this is the address," he said, pointing to a nondescript build-ing to our right.

I paid him, and Teresa and I climbed out of the cab. When we walked through the main door of the building into the reception area, a female social worker with a Jamaican accent received us with a smile and volun-teered to watch Teresa while I attended my meeting. She took Teresa's hand and tried to engage her in conversation.

"How are you Teresa?" she asked.

Teresa made no eye contact with her and ignored the question. But the social worker did not give up, trying another way to get her attention.

"Would you like to see my toys? I have lots of them."

The word "toys" got my daughter's attention and she looked at the woman fleetingly. At that point, I told her I was going for a meeting upstairs and would be back shortly. I gestured to her to follow the social worker to see the toys. As I turned and walked toward the stairs, she did not appear to mind me leaving. I had barely climbed halfway up the stairs when in my anxiety about the impending meeting, I slipped and almost fell.

"Careful, those stairs are kind of steep," the social worker cautioned from below.

Embarrassed, I straightened myself and kept climbing. Like a musical refrain in my head the words repeated: *What would they need to tell me in person? Why is this different?*

After a long, tedious climb, I entered an austere conference room. The unadorned gray-painted walls gave the room a gloomy, dismal feel, and the air was hot and stuffy. In the center of the room three women and one man were seated around a wooden table waiting for me. I slid into the only vacant chair in the ominous silence. With stone-faced expressions, the panel greeted me, and one of the women, who I believed was the leader of the group, got right to the point.

"Mrs. Zoma, your child has autism."

Her words hung there for a moment, suspended in the room. For a second I felt like I was watching myself in a movie. Then I absorbed the words with a shock, followed by immediate denial.

"No," I shook my head. "No, it can't be true."

The woman then explained that the behaviors demonstrated in the psychological evaluation were consistent with autism. As she was talking, I kept shaking my head side to side.

"No, it cannot be," I kept muttering.

Seeing my obvious distress, their expressions softened. I was convinced they had made a terrible mistake in the diagnosis and pleaded my point.

"My daughter does not have autism," I stated, with disbelief about their diagnosis. "Teresa is intelligent, healthy, vibrant, funny, happy, and energetic, and the only thing wrong is that she is not yet talking. Could it be only a language delay?" I asked, tears streaming down my face as I searched their eyes for some signal of hope.

They maintained that based on their evaluations this case was not simply a language delay. They were gentle and patient; I could sense their compassion as they watched me.

To say I was devastated would be an understatement. I felt my body go limp. I did not know much about autism spectrum disorder (ASD) at the time, but from the little I had heard, I knew it was a serious disability.

My mind went back to the only time I had heard about ASD. It had been on Barbara Walter's *20/20* news magazine on the ABC TV channel months earlier.

The program had showed some institutionalized children sitting in the corner of a sparsely furnished room, rocking continuously. They were expressionless and showed no indication of being active and playful. In fact, the reporter suggested that the children, who were described as having ASD, did nothing but rock back and forth all day long. It had caused pain in my heart that they were in an institution and not in the arms of their mothers.

Sitting now with this panel, I compared those kids with Teresa and saw no similarity. I was convinced that the evaluators must be mistaken, but was not sure what to do.

The panel members were quiet as they waited for me to recover my composure and then asked if I would be okay. I nodded slowly. One of them kindly walked me to the bilingual psychologist's office where he would explain his full report.

The psychologist, Mr. Bob Brown, a tall, soft-spoken gentleman probably in his mid-forties, explained to me that the purpose of the psychological test was to "get more information on Teresa's cognitive functioning and to assist in academic and therapeutic planning." He said that he used various assessment tools, including the Stanford-Binet Intelligence Scale: Fourth Edition, the Vineland Adaptive Behavior Scales, and the Childhood Autism Rating Scale (CARS). He had also relied on his clinical observation of Teresa and her past records, as well as his interview with me. The rest of what he told me was the same as the information in his written report, presented below:

*Test Result*
  *Estimated cognitive functioning is in the deficient range, depressed by significant behavioral interference. Teresa would not attend to picture vocabulary, identify body parts, complete a form board, or stack blocks.*

*The Vineland test was completed using the mother as the informant.*
*The following are the results:*

| Domain | Functional level |
|---|---|
| *Communication* | *Deficient* |
| *Daily Living Skills* | *Upper Deficient* |
| *Socialization* | *Deficient* |
| *Motor Skills* | *Deficient* |
| *Adaptive Composite* | *Deficient* |

In his report, the psychologist estimated Teresa's cognitive functioning to be more than two years below her chronological age.

He added, "She displayed very significant global delays and her behavioral intrusions were interfering with her overall development."

He also mentioned that The Childhood Autism Rating Scale indicated that the "overall score was suggestive of a severe level of autistic behaviors."

After all was said and done, the diagnosis was ASD. The psychologist recommended a full day, 12-month program tailored for children with special needs, in a small group of no more than five.

Other recommendations included cognitive activities, behavioral management, speech and language therapy, peer socialization, and parent support.

At the end of our meeting, Mr. Brown asked if I had any questions. Overwhelmed by this point, I had none, but accepted his business card in case I later did. He walked me downstairs to the office of the social worker attending to Teresa.

Teresa was alone in the office, although still within the social worker's view from where she was conversing with another staff member. The office was small and sparsely furnished with a little desk and file cabinet. Toys were scattered over the pale green carpet, which someone had apparently dumped on the floor from a plastic toy bin. Teresa roamed the room absentmindedly and did not acknowledge my entry. I noticed her pick up a toy, smell it, and stare at it for a moment before dropping it, only to pick up another one to repeat the ritual.

I was struck by her random acts and disengagement with objects and the fact that nothing in the room (including me) seemed to hold her attention even for a short time.

*This is odd, but it does not make her autistic*, I thought, denial resurfacing.

After a quick "thank you" to the staff, I reached out to take Teresa's hand and we walked out of the building together to begin our pilgrimage down this new and unexpected road. I felt despondent, but determined.

That was 25 years ago. It is hard to believe how time flies. I could not have imagined all that we would encounter during those years.

# Two

## Coming to America

### Nigeria
### 1988

Our story began 29 years ago in Nigeria. In the spring of 1988, my husband, Dele, and I worked at the Delta Steel Company in Ovwian-Aladja located in the present-day Delta State of Nigeria. Dele was one of many physicians that worked in the company's clinic. I worked in administration as a training officer.

Before the 1980s, Ovwian-Aladja was a rural village located in the southernmost part of Nigeria—the Niger Delta. By 1989, when we left Nigeria, this village had been transformed into a modern town, thanks to the construction in the village of the largest steel factory in Africa south of the Sahara Desert. Delta Steel Company brought new jobs and small businesses, and with those came the need for new housing developments. With new housing came new infrastructures like electricity, improved water supply, new schools and shops.

Ovwian-Aladja is also only minutes away from Warri, a major town in the Niger Delta noted for its large oil refinery as well as multinational oil companies, notably Shell and Chevron. The combined effect of the oil companies and the steel company created a flourishing local economy.

For my family, life was peaceful and good at this time. Dele and I were two of the many new-hires at the steel company. Our modern-styled two-bedroom bungalow was located inside a subdivision built and owned exclusively by the company. The locals commonly referred to this community as the "Steel Camp" or "Steel Township."

Inside the subdivision, the company built private schools for the children of staff from grades kindergarten to high school. In addition, the staff and their families had access to a fully equipped hospital with highly qualified doctors of varying specialties.

We had two beautiful and lively children, and we were excited about one more child on the way. My pregnancy was normal. I had prenatal care and did not take any medications, alcohol, or drugs during pregnancy. There were no indications that something might be wrong.

On April 26, 1988, our third child, Teresa, was born. Although she came two weeks early, she was a full-term baby, weighing 6.6 pounds. Dele's presence and participation in the birth process gave me confidence that all would be fine, and it was. The delivery was quick and uneventful.

Teresa looked healthy and beautiful, and I was filled with joy. I took her home on the third day after delivery and nursed her for about five months. She responded well to her environment and to adults who cooed over her, and she was active, with no health problems.

Commenting on her facial resemblance of me, a friend of mine said, "Finally, you got a child that looks just like you!"

I was delighted at the comment because my oldest child resembled my husband at birth and my second child took on my dad's features.

Despite Teresa's good health, I noticed something about her that was different from my two previous children: she sometimes had difficulty falling asleep at night, and cried relentlessly for no apparent reason. There appeared to be no logical explanations for her cries, such as hunger, cold, wet or dirty diapers, or gas.

I remember one night in particular when, at just two months old, she cried non-stop for several hours. It was in June 1988, and that particular evening Dele and I were getting ready for a send-off party organized in his honor by his fellow physicians. He would be leaving for the United States the following week to begin his residency training at New York Medical College.

Teresa was crying a little while we got ready, so I carried and nursed her until she was full. I then gave her a bath and handed her to her nanny who strapped Teresa to her back with a wrap, the customary way of carrying babies in Nigeria.

To get the baby to sleep, the nanny gently paced the room as she sang [1]Urhobo lullabies. On good days, this routine sent Teresa to sleep, so I kept my fingers crossed. We left for the party around 7 p.m., convinced she was falling asleep since she was quiet.

The party was expected to be short; we estimated we would be home in no more than three hours. About an hour and a half into the party, I called home to check on how things were going. I learned from the nanny that soon after we left home, Teresa had awakened and started to cry and had not stopped. We immediately left the party and when we got home Teresa was still crying. Finally, after wearing herself out from crying for seven hours, my baby fell asleep at 2 a.m.

Difficulty sleeping at night and colic behavior are not unusual for infants, as they are still trying to adjust to life outside the womb. However, Teresa's case appeared to be excessive. Most infants sleep during the day and then want to stay awake and play at night, but this was not the case with Teresa. She not only stayed wide-awake and cried at night, she did not sleep much during the day either.

On the nights that she did not cry, she still had difficulty falling asleep. She stayed in my arms, with eyes wide open. When I placed her in her crib, she protested with cries. I reported her frequent cries and lack of sleep to her pediatrician, but he found nothing wrong with her. Yet, there were many nights that no matter how hard I tried to make her go to sleep, I was unsuccessful.

---

1 Urhobo is the language spoken by the Urhobo people of the Niger Delta region of Nigeria, where I was born.

I recall one particularly stressful night. Starting from around midnight, I held Teresa in my arms and walked in circles until 5:30 a.m. before she finally fell asleep. In my red floral robe wrapped around a light cotton nightgown, I danced with her, barefoot on the light olive carpet in the spacious center of our living room. My black hair fell in many long, single braids to my shoulders and dangled on all sides of my face as I rocked and sang native lullabies to my child. For the sixtieth time, with sleep-heavy eyes, I weakly repeated a lullaby in my Uvwie-Urhobo dialect:

*Oma vie-o*   *(Baby is crying)*
*Oma vie-o*   *(Baby is crying)*

*Mo reye ke-o (Come and nurse her)*
*Mo reye Ke-o (Come and nurse her)*

*Oke share-O (Before you leave)*
*Oke share-o (Before you leave)*

*Usoni? A-A (Did you hear? Yes, Yes)*
*Usoni? A-A (Did you hear? Yes, Yes)*

The night was so still and quiet that you could hear a pin drop, until my child's cries pierced the night. In between her cries, the deafening silence became unnerving. While the repetition of the song did not put her to sleep, at least it kept the silence at bay. Although my husband and kids were sleeping in the bedrooms nearby, I could not help feeling alone. As I stared down the tender face of my crying baby, I saw how fragile and tired she looked, and I wondered, *Lord, what is wrong with my baby?*

As dawn rolled in, the stillness of the night finally came to a close when in the distance a car sped down the road, its engine roaring. My child's body was now limp and resting over my chest, her eyelids fluttering intermittently like wings of a butterfly set to perch as she gradually drifted into sleep.

The next morning I was exhausted. The whole situation overwhelmed me so much that I broke down crying. The prospect of being at my office by 8 a.m. each day had become daunting. On another occasion, when we had not slept well for about three days in a row, I showed up for work extremely tired and lethargic. Needless to say, I was not very useful after multiple nights with little or no sleep.

Other than the crying spells and sleep problems, Teresa was a happy baby. She grew normally and continued to be healthy, eating well and meeting all of the developmental milestones within the appropriate age range. At three months, she was able to hold her neck up. She sat independently at five months and crawled at around seven to eight months. She walked without support at twelve months. She also made sounds during infancy, although I do not recall specifically when I first heard the sounds.

Teresa responded with enthusiasm and laughter when her older siblings pulled or tugged at her during playtime. Whenever I picked her up and threw her up in the air, she laughed loudly and happily as I caught her in my arms. She loved being thrown into the air multiple times. As an infant, Teresa was simply a joy to have and hold.

• • •

Six months after Dele had left for the New York Medical College, it became time for the rest of the family to join him. We arrived at JFK International Airport on a wintery January night in 1989. Teresa was 8 months old, her older sister Elohor was 5 years old, and her older brother Ovie was 3 years old. We landed in a heavy snowstorm, and I remember hoping that Spain's Iberia aircraft was up for the challenge. Once safely on the ground, we taxied to our gate. The tarmac was a carpet of fresh snow and all we could do was stare at it from the cabin window, mesmerized by its beauty. The children could not wait to touch it. It was our first time seeing snow.

Although I knew it was going to be cold, nothing prepared me for the cold wind that blasted us when we left the airport building for our car. My naiveté about how harshly cold New York City could be in January was evident in the way I had dressed my kids. I had clothed them in only sweat suits made from a rather light material, something suitable for cool Nigerian weather. They wore no inner layers, no sweaters, no coats, and no hats, gloves, or scarves. Thank goodness, Dele had guessed we would not be dressed for the weather so he came prepared, though regrettably, all the paraphernalia and heavy coats that he brought did nothing to protect us from the biting cold. We shivered like leaves in the wind. Coming from a hot, tropical climate, I wondered how the people here survived; it was simply brutal. For a moment, I feared we might not survive it.

Dele drove us to our apartment on Steinway Street in Astoria, Queens. During the entire ride from the airport, I sat stiffly in the car, frozen by the cold and unable to move my mouth to speak. I felt pain in my ears. I worried about my children. It was a gloomy ride home. So much for the excitement of coming to New York, New York!

About two weeks after we arrived in New York City, the children and I were curious to see the outside of our small apartment, so we ventured out for fresh air. We had barely walked a block from our apartment building when we made a 180-degree turn and literally ran back home to escape the fierce, icy wind.

My son, Ovie said, "My ears hurt Mommy!"

"Me too!" said my older daughter, Elohor.

I could not feel my nose and my lips were numb. "Children, come on! We need to head back home!" I told them. We ran for our dear lives!

Back in our warm and modest one-bedroom apartment, we remained inside as much as we could for two months. We did not venture out until March when the frosty weather had mercifully relented.

# Three

## Not a Typical Toddler

## New York City
## 1991

In 1991, Steinway Street, in the heart of Astoria, Queens, was a bustling shopping hub. Along both sides of the street were national chain stores situated side by side with local family owned shops, some of which have been serving this culturally diverse community for decades.

The street's five-block business district housed everything from hardware, antiques, furnishings, electronics, clothing, and shoes, to eyewear and jewelry. Attorney offices, banks, flower shops, Delis/Bakeries, salons, medical/dental offices, liquor stores, real estate businesses, and a host of restaurants, cafes and specialty food stores were also part of the shopping experience in this vibrant community.

Enthusiastic shoppers crowded the streets and sidewalks looking for bargains, while passing vehicles wove through them in the traffic congestion. No matter what day of the week it was, or what time of day, the street was bustling with activity.

Our apartment was on the second floor of a three-story building. Below it was a travel agency owned by our landlords, a Greek-born couple. I still remember the pretty rose-colored carpet that lined the entire floor of the apartment, with matching rose and white lacey drapes.

Our home was practical in furnishings, yet intimate and beautiful. The best part was that it was small and easy to clean and maintain. Considering all of the dramatic change we encountered in coming to a new country, it was grounding to have a simple, comfortable place to call home.

● ● ●

As a toddler growing up on Steinway Street, Teresa was cute, happy, and boisterous, just like many children her age. But it was the uncommon or odd behaviors that she displayed for much of the day that remain indelible in my memory, and caused me to question her development.

One of these atypical behaviors was her eating habit. When served food of any kind on a plate, she turned the plate over, emptying its contents onto the floor. She then leaned forward to smell the food. Finally, she proceeded to eat the food from the floor.

Though she was a joyful eater, her food repertoire was quite limited and consisted mainly of rice, bread, cornflakes, and meat. She ate these foods in a peculiar way. For instance, she always ate her cornflakes dry, preferring not to add milk. Then she drank the milk separately afterwards.

What I found even more idiosyncratic was the way she ate her bread. She preferred to eat only the crust of the bread. She would peel the surrounding crust off a slice of bread and eat it. Then she would discard the center of the bread.

Whenever we could get Teresa to eat with us at the table, her table manner fell short and was a source of amusement for me. During dinners, she frequently grabbed pieces of meat from other people's plate without asking. Her older siblings learned their lesson the hard way when their pieces of meat disappeared without warning. Subsequently, Elohor and Ovie began to hustle for the seat situated away from Teresa during dinner time. It was hard for me not to laugh when I watched the dynamics of the children as they tried to avoid the "meat grabber" who insisted on sitting next to them, and followed them as they tried to move away from her. While Teresa fully expected to share her siblings' food and other things like toys, she was unwilling to share hers. When she acquired a little language, one of the phrases that she used more frequently than others was "no share."

Teresa also showed signs of extreme hyperactivity. Active and energetic from dawn until dusk, she was constantly snacking, playing, and moving. Her favorite things to do were body flips and somersaults. She flipped endlessly on the living room couch and all over the floor, all day long. She was also an enthusiastic runner. Running outside was one thing, but running inside a small, cramped apartment such as ours was another.

One evening, while the family was sitting around in the living room watching TV, Teresa came from nowhere with hands stretched out and did a short sprint toward the TV, causing the 32-inch screen to crash to the floor with a very loud sound. Unperturbed by the chaos she had caused, she turned around and walked away to continue her play. It struck me as odd that she did not appear to be concerned by the crash.

In addition to her hyperactivity, her language development was significantly delayed, and as a consequence, she had limited means to communicate with people. When called, she did not respond to her name. An outsider might have thought she was deaf, but I knew she was not deaf because she often danced to commercial jingles on TV.

By age three, she still had not developed functional language- the ability to use language meaningfully, as opposed to spitting out words that neither make sense nor convey any real communicative intent. Occasionally, she passively blurted out words without paying attention to them. The words she blurted out were mostly words she had heard on TV shows. For example, she tried to imitate, in a parrot-like manner, words from the popular children's TV show, *Sesame Street*.

My daughter loved *Sesame Street*! During the show's opening song, Teresa often swung her body from side to side dancing, and then attempted to repeat some of the words the characters said or sang. She repeated numbers like, "one, two, three, four, five, nine and ten," from a song on counting, skipping some numbers and mispronouncing others. Many of the words she spoke were mere approximations of the actual word, but one could tell what number she was attempting to repeat. She continued to wiggle and dance as she counted on, her eyes fixed to the TV. It was joyful to watch!

Through all of her spontaneous dashes, flips, turns, and somersaults, she barely communicated or interacted with any one of us at home through speech. She did not even engage in play with her siblings. For the most part, she made no eye contact and ignored all of us except when she needed something from us. In order to make her needs known to me, she held my hand and led me to her object of interest. She then stared at or pointed to the object. When I held the target object, she snagged it from my hand and walked away without making any eye contact or acknowledging me in any way.

The combination of hyperactivity and language development delay had ramifications outside of the home. Whenever we went to church, she did not act appropriately. She made loud noises and walked all over the pews, to the distraction of the other worshippers. She also did not seem to understand the concept of personal space and would often walk into people aimlessly. I usually ended up taking her outside the church for most of the service, where we hung out with other mothers with crying infants. At over two years old, Teresa was usually the oldest child outside. Eventually, we stopped going to church.

Teresa displayed other atypical behaviors, and one of these was particularly troubling to me. She loved to eat paint from the walls around the house. She would position her teeth on the edge of a wall and bite or scrape it. Then she would eat the paint that got in her mouth. It did not matter how many times I tried to pull her away, she always went back to the wall as soon as she found an opportunity. I feared that she might develop lead poisoning because we lived in a fairly old building in which paint containing lead may have been used. To my relief, when she was later tested by a pediatric neurologist, the test result was negative.

Another odd behavior had to do with the way she walked. She walked on her toes all the time, whether barefoot or wearing shoes. She never let her heels touch the ground. She even ran on her toes.

However, the behavior that most caused me to think that something might be seriously wrong with my child had to do with her extreme tantrums. Teresa threw so many huge tantrums that going out with her became a tremendous challenge. A trip to the store or merely passing by a store was one of the most difficult trips to make. This was because she wanted to buy everything she liked. She made a big fuss if she did not get her way.

Although it is common for children to throw tantrums when their parents tell them they can't have their wish, Teresa's protests were explosive. She cried, kicked, screamed, and threw herself to the floor, while many customers watched in wonder. Her siblings stood by with embarrassment as I stared down at her helplessly, unable to calm her tirade.

I vividly recall one tantrum in front of a small Greek-owned convenience store located on the corner of Steinway and Ditmars Boulevard. We walked past the store daily to drop off and pick up my two older kids from school. It was tough for Teresa to pass by the store and not go in because she knew it housed her favorite things: candies. Most of the time when we passed by and she indicated her wish to go into the store, I was successful in redirecting her attention away from it. However, there were days that no matter what I did to get her to look away, I was unable to. Therefore, as a precaution, I held her hand firmly whenever we got near the storefront to prevent her from running in.

On this particular afternoon, we were on our way to pick up her siblings from school. Teresa was seemingly calm, happy to be dressed in her favorite pink t-shirt. About two yards from the store, she spotted the candy aisle inside. The allure of mini Skittles, her favorite candy, ignited her desire to go in, and quickly became overpowering. In a split second, she slipped from my grasp and bolted toward the open double-glass door.

She already had one foot inside when I caught her left hand. She yanked it free and took two more steps inside the store, by this time, facing the center aisle, which had all of the candies and sweets. I caught her left hand again and held it firmly, quickly surveying the small store and feeling instant relief when there were no other customers inside. No worries about being embarrassed.

The store was tiny. Two other aisles to the right of us displayed potato chips, cookies, peanuts, water bottles and an assortment of sodas. More temptation. Against the wall at the far right, the refrigerator held cold drinks, juice, milk and other tantalizing beverages.

The owner of the store was a kind, middle-aged Greek man. Glancing our way from behind the counter to our left, he returned to his paper work, unconcerned by the commotion we had caused. He knew us well. It was not our first time there.

Despite my firmness, my child pulled me further into the store. She was not crying, just serious and resolute about what she wanted.

"No candy today", I said, as I tried to lead her out of the store.

She resisted and struggled to cut loose of my hold, but I was able to maneuver her out of the store. Once outside, she threw herself on the sidewalk and began to wail. She rolled and kicked and screamed in protest as I stared down with my usual helplessness.

I wanted to just give up and succumb to her demands. It could have been easier for me. But then my child would not understand that if one buys candy today, one does not need to buy it tomorrow, and I would have to succumb every time we passed by. Instead, I thought about outsmarting her by changing our route to the school; however, there were no other routes without candy stores. In fact, the other side of the street had two or three candy stores. There was no way out.

The pavement where my child fell stretched about four yards from the store to the edge of the road, so she had ample space to roll and kick. I watched her with confusion as she screamed her heart out.

*This could not be normal, could it?* I wondered.

Coming from a large extended family, I've seen numerous children grow from toddlers to pre-teens and into adulthood, and not one respond to a simple "no" like my child. Of course most children feel disappointed when their request is turned down by their parents, and some may even throw a fit or two, but nothing like what I was experiencing with Teresa.

My child's shoes flew off in two different directions as she kicked. She was so loud that a few passersby across the street looked our way momentarily and then hurried on their way. I worried that they may be judging me. *What do they know?* I shrugged the thought off my mind.

I tried to divert Teresa's attention by naming other things she liked that we had at home. I threw out words like ice cream, pizza, and meat, and used gestures to make her understand that she could have these things when we got home. At this point, my plea fell on deaf ears.

After what seemed like an eternity, she still did not budge, so I picked her up, placed her over my shoulders, and trudged the four blocks to the school. As I carried her, she continued to kick and cry loudly in protest, making my progress laborious, but by the time we arrived at the school, she had calmed down. She walked home by my side without any further incident.

Another episode that I recall happened at a Payless Shoe store on Steinway Street. This particular day was a bright and sunny Saturday afternoon, and the street was, as usual, filled with people. It was an ideal day to take the children for a walk, have ice cream, and window shop. The outing started off well, with Teresa cooperating, so I thought it just might be one of our good days out.

Pushing my luck, I took the children into Payless. Long racks of shoes stretched from the front of the store to the far back, all organized and clearly labeled for size, gender, and age. Upon entry into the crowded store, my two older children, Elohor and Ovie, fanned out into different directions of interest. I asked Teresa to stay with me but she declined and went off on her own. I took note of the direction she was walking to as I moved to the women's aisle.

I browsed the size 10 section. Nothing caught my fancy until I spotted a pair of leather sandals. I tried them on but they didn't fit. After trying a second pair of leather sandals with the same result, I decided to leave for another store.

I found Elohor and Ovie and told them it was time to go. They went obediently toward the door and waited for me. Teresa was standing by a shoe rack close to the door. When I reached out to take her hand, she yanked her hand from my hold and bolted back toward the interior of the store. I waited to see what she wanted to do. Soon enough, she returned with a pair of shoes, and from her manner, I knew she wanted them. I didn't have money to buy the shoes. Besides, even if I'd had money, she did not need a new pair of shoes.

However, because of her communication deficit, Teresa did not understand any of that logic and trying to reason with her was fruitless. I gently took the shoes from her and told her we could not get them that day. True to form, she went down on the floor and yelled and cried as fellow shoppers gawked. Again, I had to hoist her up on my shoulders, and my other kids and I prematurely and reluctantly walked back home.

● ● ●

Teresa's early childhood years was a mixed bag. On the one hand, she had difficulty following directions, was inattentive, hyperactive, and threw numerous tantrums. On the other hand, she was funny, exuberant, adventurous, and a joy to hug and hold. I love her with all my heart. She was and still is a real gem.

Going to the playground was always a thrill for her, because it gave her a chance to feel free. She enjoyed running around and jumping endlessly with no restrictions. It was a pleasure to see her so happy. She wasn't scared of exploring all the different structures and activities available in the playground and climbed on everything within her reach without fear or assistance. She loved adventure and took risks. It was obvious that the playground was very much her forte.

I found myself bursting out in laughter at some of the funny things that she did. She loved to dance. In the middle of climbing or running, she would stop instantly, and wiggle her tiny waist in a spontaneous dance move. Then just as suddenly as she started to dance, she would stop and continue to climb or run, only to repeat the dance ritual again minutes later. When that happened, I could tell she was having the time of her life!

# Four

## New York City
## 1992

By Teresa's third birthday, she still had not begun to talk and I grew very concerned. Before then, I was not too worried because my two older children had both started talking later than normal. Elohor was well over 2 years old before she said anything meaningful, and Ovie was close to 3 years old before he first uttered a complete sentence. I therefore saw Teresa's case as part of a pattern set by my first two children.

However, when she was not talking by her third birthday, I had a strong feeling that something was not right. Although she had made sounds as an infant, her first word, "no," did not emerge until she was halfway through her second year. Subsequent to that, she had only developed a few vocabulary words. By age 3, I estimated that the number of words she used, with pronunciation that was not exactly intelligible, was about 10, almost all of which were food items, including peanut butter, rice, orange juice, and ice cream. She also said, "no," and "go." She knew the words "mommy" and "daddy" and recognized to whom those terms referred, but did not address us directly using the terms. She did not call her siblings by their names either.

Mostly nonverbal, my child communicated primarily through gestures. Her repertoire of words consisted mostly of echolalia, whereby she repeated what other people had said, sometimes immediately after and at other times hours, days, or even weeks later.

For example, a friend of mine once said "hello" to us as we walked by one Saturday morning. Teresa neither replied nor acknowledged my friend in any way until 10 minutes later, when she muttered "hello" to herself. Like a parrot, she repeated this word many more times during the course of that day and for many days after that.

Shortly after Teresa's third birthday, I spent some time reflecting upon her communication ability and her readiness to learn. First, I recognized her strengths. I noticed that she liked to watch her favorite TV shows and movies repeatedly for long periods of time while imitating words, songs, and gestures.

From *Sesame Street*, she learned to count to 10 and to recite parts of the alphabet, albeit in a meaningless singsong manner. She appeared to sing along with the main character Maria in *The Sound of Music*, although her words were unintelligible. And she was mesmerized by the Tin Man in *The Wizard of Oz* and imitated his gestures. She particularly loved the Tin Man's song, "If Only I Had a Heart." I think the first verse goes something like this:

*When a man's an empty kettle*
*He should be on his mettle*
*And yet I'm torn apart*
*Just because I'm presumin'*
*That I could be kinda human*
*If I only had a heart*

*(Next verse)*

*I'd be tender, I'd be gentle*
*And awful sentimental*

*Regarding love and art*
*I'd be friends with the sparrows*
*And the boy that shoots the arrows*
*If I only had a heart*

It was a thrill to observe Teresa watch the Tin Man. She never sat down to see the entire movie but when her favorite parts came up, she stood still and watched. Dorothy's discovery of the Tin Man was one of her favorite scenes. As soon as she saw Dorothy crawl toward the foot of the Tin Man and tap on it with her knuckles, my child would begin to giggle with excitement. Then she'd watch with rapt attention as Dorothy and the Scarecrow try to get the Tin Man to talk by lubricating him with oil.

When the Tin Man began to talk, my child would jump for joy. When Dorothy banged on his chest, my child would block out the resulting sound with her two hands on her ears. Again she would giggle with excitement.

"It's empty," the Tin Man says. "The tin smith forgot to give me a heart."

"No heart?" asks Dorothy.

"No heart!" the Tin Man repeats.

Each time, Teresa would repeat "no heart" and she would laugh so hard you would think she was being tickled excitedly. When the Tin Man actually began to sing, my child was exhilarated. She would copy his strides and hops and beat her chest whenever the Tin Man did so.

In retrospect, it strikes me as heartbreakingly apropos that Teresa strongly identified with the Tin Man. When his mouth was rusted shut, my child was, at the time, trapped in her own isolated world, unable to communicate through speech. She also shared the Tin Man's difficulty connecting with others emotionally, though she had plenty of heart.

Although these strengths for learning readiness encouraged me, she displayed many significant obstacles to learning that were worrisome. Her ability to sustain attention to and imitate words and songs were strengths, yet she did those only when she was watching a favorite movie or show. At other times, she was fleetingly attentive and showed no interest in people or learning situations.

I observed that she related to others and objects in inconsistent and inappropriate ways. For example, if she wanted something that someone had, she would come by and grab it from that person. She did not understand courtesy and had difficulty following rules and adhering to boundaries. Self-absorbed, she appeared indifferent to people and oblivious to her surroundings.

She did not demonstrate empathy, even when a family member was in distress. For example, once when she saw me crying, she walked away from me without acknowledging my emotion or even making eye contact. Although she allowed us to hug her, she made no attempt to sustain the hugs and did not initiate any of them. Most of the time, she walked away from our attempts to hold or hug her.

Then there were her tantrums which were detailed in the previous chapter. In addition, she sometimes pounded her toys and other objects on the ground, destroying them in the process.

These challenges concerning Teresa's behavior and development were very disturbing; however, when I shared my worries with relatives and friends, they assured me that she was going to be fine. They believed that what I was seeing was simply a case of language delay and reminded me that every child was different, and every child had his or her own timeline. When I called my mother in Nigeria, she told me that we had a relative whose daughter did not speak until she was 5 years old. When she started to speak, she became a chatterbox.

I prayed and hoped that my child would turn out just like that relative's daughter. I wanted to believe these reassurances, but the mother in me instinctively knew that my child was not just a case of language delay.

So, I took my concern to her pediatrician who told me that typically by the age of three, children would have developed language skills. According to the physician, an evaluation was in order, and the first thing to do was to rule out hearing loss. For that reason, she ordered a hearing test for Teresa and referred us to the Queens College Speech-Language-Hearing Center in Flushing, New York.

We did not get an appointment immediately because of the long waiting list; however, on March 12, 1992, just before her fourth birthday, Teresa was given an initial hearing screening that was inconclusive. The clinician referred her for further evaluation.

Three months later, on June 30, 1992, the second audiological evaluation was done. Right after the evaluation, the audiologist, a soft-spoken Asian woman, probably in her late twenties or early thirties, told me the results of her evaluation.

Much of what she said was professional jargon, so I asked for the bottom line. She said Teresa was not deaf and her hearing was within normal range. It was not news to me. I always knew she was not deaf because I had seen her dance to music on TV many times. However, I understood it was standard procedure for the evaluation to be done.

Teresa was also given a speech and language evaluation at the same center by Ms. Ann Smith, the speech pathologist. Teresa did not respond to Ms. Smith's pleasant greeting when she came to meet us in the waiting room, but willingly accompanied her to the evaluation room. I followed behind them.

The floor of the speech pathologist's room was filled with different objects and toys that could catch the interest of young children. Dolls, a play comb and brush, stuffed animals, toy cars, plates, cups and spoons littered the floor. Ms. Smith's objective was to observe Teresa at play and to try to interact with her.

Teresa paid little or no attention to the objects or toys. She also did not acknowledge my presence or Ms. Smith's presence in any way. Instead, she moved freely around the room picking up or reaching for any object within view and then dropping it seconds after, only to reach out for another object. At one point she noticed her reflection in a mirror on the wall and watched herself for a short time as she moved back and forth in front of the mirror.

With the exception of this mirror, she attended to objects for only a few seconds at a time, indiscriminately putting them in her mouth and biting them. Although she uttered some words during the session, she was inattentive to the clinician and did not respond to whatever Ms. Smith said, while I watched with apprehension. I was thinking about the fact that my daughter was 4 years old.

A couple of weeks later, I received the report. It was late morning and my husband was at work. Teresa's two siblings were in the bedroom playing. I sat on the couch with the manila envelope that was addressed to me. Beside me, Teresa was doing her usual flips and somersaults on the couch, but I paid no attention to her. My hands trembled as I undid the clasp of the envelope, although I was not sure exactly why. I read the first line of the report, and the second, and the third, fishing for some good news, some hope, some sort of reassurance. When I got to where it said that my child presented with "profound receptive/expressive language impairment," my heart dropped. I turned to look at my precious baby flipping and tumbling joyfully beside me.

*She is so happy*, I thought. *She may not be talking, but at least she is happy*, I consoled myself.

Her joyful, carefree attitude was a source of comfort for me at that moment.

The revelation was grim. I read the report meticulously, trying to make sense of the professional jargon while coming to the realization that my child's language problem was profound. Excerpts of the report read:

*In the assessment of her language skills, Teresa presented with profound receptive/expressive language impairment.*

*Due to her behavior, language comprehension skills were assessed informally through observation, and they were judged to be profoundly impaired.*

*With the exception of inconsistent response to the form "no," she did not respond to any linguistic input or her name.*

*For the most part, she did not initiate or maintain interaction with the adults in the room.*

*Communicative acts were exhibited infrequently and appeared to be limited to requesting objects/actions and protesting.*

*Although she vocalized throughout the session, vocalization did not appear to carry any communicative intent.*

Based on the evaluation result, Ms. Smith recommended the following:

1. A blood test to rule out lead poisoning.
2. A complete psychological and neurological evaluation to gain more specific information regarding Teresa's cognitive and neurological functioning.
3. Placement in a pre-school program for language-impaired children.
4. Speech-language therapy at least twice weekly on an individual basis, to begin as soon as possible.

It was a devastating blow for me to read the report. It bothered me greatly that my child was "profoundly impaired" in most of the major areas of language. Even though I knew something was wrong with her communication ability, I had always been hopeful that the prognosis would not be as shattering.

In a deeply sincere and solemn conversation with the speech pathologist, Ms. Smith informed me that at age four, we had started this process late. She revealed that the earlier an intervention started, the higher the chance of a positive outcome, and that intervention could have been started for Teresa as early as 18 months. Her revelation generated "what if" questions that followed me for years to come. What if I had known this fact? How would my child's life be different? Even to this day, I still wonder.

I have spent a long time looking back to see what I might have missed, yet, I do not see how I would have known something was seriously wrong with my child by 18 months. She had met all of her developmental milestones-sitting up, crawling, standing, walking-and she was active, healthy, and exuberant. The fact that she was not talking by 18 months struck me as not typical compared with other children, but when I compared her with my two older children, who also did not talk by that age, I thought nothing of it. Her tantrums did not show until she was much older.

Following the report, Ms. Smith contacted the Early Childhood Direction Center in Queens, New York, and provided them with all of Teresa's information. The center would help me find speech-language services for Teresa. We were also placed on the waiting list for speech services at the Queens College Speech-Language-Hearing Center, and referred to the Special Education Department in Queens, where a complete psychological and neurological evaluation would be conducted as soon as possible.

From then on, everything happened quickly. Within a week, the special education department sent me the necessary consent forms to fill out, which I signed and mailed back immediately. Shortly after they received the forms, the department scheduled a multi-faceted evaluation. This included another speech and language evaluation, physical functioning (fine and gross motor), and psychological and social-emotional evaluations. These evaluations were carried out at the office of the special education department in Queens.

This round of speech and language evaluations confirmed the results of the first one, and gave me an idea of the age level at which my child was functioning. The findings indicated a severe language disorder/delay. According to the report, Teresa's Receptive Communication Age (the age at which she receives and responds to messages) and Expressive Communication Age (the age at which she expresses messages) were 12 months. In other words, she was operating as a 1 year old, even though she was 4 years of age.

Following the report, the speech therapist recommended one-on-one speech therapy twice a week, for 30 minutes per session.

The result of the physical functioning evaluation indicated that Teresa demonstrated age-appropriate gross and fine motor skills. Her socio-emotional status was also found to be adequate.

Of all of the evaluations done, the most significant one was the psychological, because it gave a diagnosis of what was going on with my baby. Now I could understand why they needed to share this information with me in person on that unforgettable day at the gloomy conference room of the special education department office in Queens, New York.

•  •  •

Although the experts had told me their opinion, I decided to seek a second opinion. My quest took Teresa and me to the Elmhurst Hospital in New York City to see a child neurologist. I told him that the psychologist had diagnosed Teresa with autism spectrum disorder (ASD) but I needed a second opinion.

He examined Teresa and then asked me questions regarding her communication, behavior, and self-help abilities. At the end of our session, the neurologist confirmed Teresa's diagnosis to be ASD but to be confident, he ordered a blood test to rule out lead poisoning. The result came out negative.

I asked about doing a brain scan, but he told me that a CAT scan was not necessary because the diagnosis of ASD was clear. After this confirmation by the neurologist, I finally accepted the diagnosis.

In the following months, I plunged myself into reading everything I could find about this brain dysfunction afflicting my daughter. I was surprised that I could not find many books to read about autism. Child psychiatrist Leo Kanner, a doctor at Johns Hopkins, published a paper on autism in 1943, and German scientist Hans Asperger had identified the condition known as Asperger's syndrome about the same time.[i] Yet, here it was the early '90s, and there were still very few books to read on autism. So, I read a number of medical periodicals and journals that

I got from the library on research relating to autism in Europe and around the world. The studies documented specific symptoms that were common among certain children who had conditions that we now know as autism. With research information about ASD still unfolding, there were several other studies, but nothing written in understandable form for parents and educators who wanted to know more about the condition, and more importantly, what to do to help their child or student. I am happy to note that today, that is no longer the case. There are now many helpful resources about autism both on professional websites and in books.

A pivotal book that I did find was by Dr. Bernard Rimland called *Infantile Autism: The Syndrome and Its Implications for a Neural Theory of Behavior.* An article about him in the *New York Times* best describes what I learned from his book:

> When his young son, Mark, received a diagnosis of autism, doctors generally blamed the disorder on cold, distant mothering. In his book *Infantile Autism: The Syndrome and Its Implications for a Neural Theory of Behavior,* Dr. Rimland demolished the cold-mother theory by presenting lucid evidence that the disorder was rooted in biology.[ii]

I cannot describe how relieved I felt when I read this.

*At least somebody understands,* I thought gratefully.

Even then, I still made conscious efforts and proactively hugged Teresa every chance I had during the day to reassure myself that even if there was an atom of truth in these falsities, I would not be guilty of "cold mothering." But the more I wanted to hug my child, the more she disregarded me and walked away.

The *Times* article goes on to note:

> "[Rimland] was tremendously important to the field, in that he reoriented research from a focus on the parents to a focus on the

brain," Dr. Fred R. Volkmar, director of the Child Study Center at Yale, said. "He also developed the first checklist for diagnosing autism. He was a pathfinder and tireless advocate for families dealing with autism."[iii]

My reading of Dr. Rimland's book re-affirmed my increasing acceptance of Teresa's diagnosis. My initial doubt about the correctness of the diagnosis had hinged on the fact Teresa did not look like the children with autism that I had seen on TV. Furthermore, unlike the manner in which children with autism were portrayed in the media at the time, Teresa was not a quiet, sad, inactive, and withdrawn child. Although she ignored people around her, she enjoyed her own company and was visibly happy and vibrant. She was a boisterous burst of energy as she ran, jumped, twirled, and body-flipped all day long.

Though I felt reluctant, I realized that I had to look beyond my child's seeming normalcy. I pondered on my discussion with the psychologist who evaluated her. He had explained to me that children with ASD share a common thread that included deficits in social communication and restricted interests. But he also said that ASD affected each person in different ways, and could range from very mild to severe, making it a spectrum disorder. Looking back, it became clear to me that Teresa showed the same deficits in social communication and restricted interests as other children with autism. What was different about her was that she presented on the mild to medium side of the spectrum.

The psychologist had also named other facts generally associated with ASD, most of which Teresa exhibited. They included the following:

- *Children with ASD might not respond to their names by 12 months.*
- *They might not play "pretend" games by 18 months.*
- *They might avoid eye contact and want to be alone.*
- *They might have trouble understanding other people's feelings or talking about their own feelings.*
- *They might have delayed speech and language skills.*

- *They repeat words or phrases over and over (echolalia).*
- *They might give unrelated answers to questions.*
- *They might get upset by minor changes.*
- *They might have obsessive interests.*
- *They might flap their hands, rock their bodies, or spin in circles.*
- *They might have unusual reactions to the way things sound, smell, taste, look, or feel.*

When I questioned him further, the psychologist mentioned that there was currently no medical test to diagnose ASD; therefore, diagnosis was made based on observation and the child's development.

Furthermore, he revealed that ASD, which occurs in all racial, ethnic, and socioeconomic groups, is often diagnosed before the age of three and lasts throughout a person's lifetime. He shared that statistics indicate ASD to be more prevalent in boys than in girls and there is currently no cure for the condition.

For many days and weeks following the evaluations, I thought about all of the information I had received and learned. I was surprised and grateful to discover that I was not overcome with worries, but felt an inner strength that manifested in my quiet resolve to rise above the fear and the unknown. I resolved to do whatever it took to help my child reach her God-given potential, whatever that might be. I felt a stoic resignation to our challenges, yet a strong desire to change the things that were within my control, and, my daughter's attitude helped to reinforce my resolve. When she was not throwing a fit about something, she was a happy, curious, funny bone of a young girl who brought me joy each day.

# Five

## New York City
## 1992

"You're going to school today," I whispered with delight to Teresa. It was the summer of 1992. Teresa, age 4, was going to start preschool at the Interdisciplinary Center for Child Development in Bayside, New York. It was finally beginning—the educational intervention that I hoped would eventually help my child develop essential life skills, especially speech. Of course I would be lying if I said I wasn't also looking forward to some free time to myself for the first time in years. I could maybe watch some TV shows uninterrupted for the first time since she was born.

At my words, Teresa looked at me fleetingly then turned away. This was her usual behavior. She ignored people most of the time, although she knew how to take their hand and walk them to objects of interest. Right now, standing in our living room, she was more interested in her new outfit and lunch box that we had bought the day before. She would not take her eyes off her pink Cinderella lunch box, and looked adorable in her new blue jeans, yellow t-shirt, and purple sweater. Like any mother on her child's first day of school, I was nervous, proud, and excited. I paced in and out of the living room doing little chores to keep myself busy while waiting for the school bus to arrive.

The school was a long drive from our home in Queens, and it would be the first time Teresa would leave home without me. I was worried about how she was going to cope with the transition, so I decided to ride with her in the special yellow school bus provided by the school district. I don't know if Teresa understood what "school" meant, but so far she appeared to be willing to follow me to wherever I was taking her that morning, walking calmly beside me down to the curb.

When we climbed into the bus, there were already two other kids on the bus, both boys I noticed. They sat quietly, one of them half asleep. I closely watched Teresa's reaction as we rode along in the bus. As she sat by me strapped into her seat, she appeared to be enjoying the sights, gazing through the window at the early morning traffic.

Before long the bus driver stopped to pick up another student. This child was crying as his mother walked him toward the bus, and he continued to cry while his mom lifted him into the bus and the bus aide strapped him into his seat. He did not show any resistance. He just cried. None of the children in the bus, including Teresa, looked in the direction of the crying boy. They appeared oblivious to him. Teresa continued her focus on the street's sights and sounds as she gazed through the window.

When we got to the school, only Teresa and I got off the bus; so, I figured the other kids were going to a different school. Teresa walked confidently by my side into the inviting, well-maintained school building, holding my hand with her right hand and clutching her pretty pink lunch box with her left.

The front door of the building opened up into a narrow hallway from which several offices branched out. With no trouble I located the office of the school secretary who greeted us and called Teresa by her first name, commenting on how cute she looked. I felt immediately comfortable not only due to the cleanliness of the building, but also because of the secretary's warm demeanor. She knew my daughter's name before I told her, which indicated they were prepared for her arrival. That simple fact also put me at ease. I felt confident that Teresa was at the right place.

Her pre-school classroom was exclusively for children with ASD. The room had six students in all, including Teresa. Again, she was the only female student in the room, which seemed to support the statistics I had read about that indicated that ASD was more common in boys than girls. In fact, the current ratio of boys to girls, of children with ASD in the United States, is about 5:1.[iv]

A tall, smiling young teacher named Flora welcomed us, and again called Teresa by her name. She introduced Teresa to the rest of the class, who hardly paid any attention to us. She then proceeded to show Teresa how to place her jacket in a small closet and her treasured lunch box in her own cubby.

Curious to see how the students were taught, I decided to sit in the corner of the classroom to watch while the teacher conducted class. My eyes wandered around, taking in the environment, which, like the downstairs offices, impressed me. As I surveyed the room, the first thing I noticed was some brightly-colored children's artwork pinned to a bulletin board. Tiny tables and chairs were placed in groups around the room. There were two large, colorful rugs—one with the numbers 1–20 and the other with the 26 letters of the alphabet. Books and stuffed animals were tucked in different locations and colorful daily schedules hung in easily visible places.

As I watched, the children rotated through various learning/play stations. In the block-building center, students stacked and rearranged a variety of colorful blocks, attempting to build objects. The benefit of this center is to give students the opportunity to interact with each other as they explore the blocks together. In addition, the students learn socially acceptable ways to express their thoughts and feelings in the process of sharing and cooperating.

In the art center, students had access to crayons and drawing paper. They were mostly engaged in exploration rather than drawing or coloring. Some drew random circles or lines on their paper, changing crayons spontaneously without any clear focus. However, the benefit of this activity is that the children are using and developing their fine motor skills. This in turn will enhance their writing skills when they are ready to write.

In the puzzles center, children manipulated puzzle pieces. This activity helps with hand-eye coordination, fine motor skills, and even logical thinking skills.

I noticed the teacher moving around each center and trying to listen in and encourage interaction between the students. She asked probing questions sometimes and would tap one of the students to respond in speech or sign language.

The students later moved to circle time where they sang songs and learned body parts like the head, eyes, nose, and ears.

I went in and out of the classroom until the end of the school day. After dismissal, we bade our goodbyes and took our bus ride back home. The first day of school came and went without incident!

The ride back to the apartment was quiet. Teresa may have been physically and mentally tired because she was not used to the cognitive activities to which she had been exposed that day.

As for me, I did not do much thinking during the ride. I even dozed off for a short while. I usually have a hard time dozing off because Teresa keeps me alert always, so, subconsciously, my nerves must have finally relaxed. After our positive first day of school, I came away with a good feeling about the whole experience. Any vestiges of nervousness that I once felt about my child's transition to school began to slip away.

The next morning, Teresa did not resist when I dressed her for school. I did not plan to accompany her to school this time and that made me a little uneasy. Thinking she might cry, I braced myself. We climbed down the stairway leading from our apartment and walked toward the waiting bus. Teresa went confidently to the bus and climbed in before the bus aide could even reach her. I stood and watched as she hopped onto a seat by the window. Then she turned to me and smiled as she waved goodbye.

"See you later baby," I said as I gave her a thumbs-up. She smiled even wider. At that moment, I knew I would have nothing to worry about.

MY first day alone at the apartment was surprisingly not so different from the other days. Although I enjoyed the luxury of a longer shower, still, I had clothes to launder, groceries to pick up, food to prepare, and some errands to run, including the post office and the dry cleaner's. I did all of these in a hurry so that I could pick up my other two children from school and get them started on their homework before Teresa arrived. Before I knew it, the day was gone. I remember asking myself, *"Where did the hours go?"*

# Six

## PRESCHOOL CURRICULUM

## New York City
## 1992

Teresa's pre-school program was impressive. There were three adults (one teacher and two aides) for a total of six kids, creating a 1:2 ratio of adults to students. The teacher used a number of developmentally appropriate interventions specifically geared toward the learning challenges associated with autism. For instance, the curriculum placed a great deal of emphasis on basic life and social skills such as communicating needs, waiting and taking turns, sharing, and playing with peers.

These skills were taught with a great deal of multi-sensory inputs. Auditory learning included electronic devices like a tape recorder to play learning or action songs. Action songs were used to encourage and teach self-help skills like brushing teeth. Each child had a spare toothbrush in school with which to practice. Action songs were also used to learn the names of peers and the function of the telephone, as well as the alphabet, numbers, and body parts.

Furthermore, the kids participated in many kinesthetic and hands-on activities that involved a lot of movement and exploration of toys and objects.

Instruction also made much use of visuals; for instance, when the teacher mentioned an object such as a ball, she simultaneously showed the children a real ball so they could make the connection between the word and the object.

These multi-sensory activities helped to increase Teresa's ability to look, pay attention, and participate in learning activities.

In order to communicate with these mostly nonverbal learners, the educators used a combination of gestures, sign language, natural language, symbols, and picture exchange. With picture exchange, the students were taught to hand a picture of an object they desired to their teacher. That single action told the teacher what they wanted without the children having to utter a word. Teresa and her peers also received group and individual speech therapy sessions from a licensed speech pathologist who came into the classroom.

In order to foster communication, different parts of the room were labeled for different activities; and, there was a picture-based schedule that showed, in sequence, all the various activities for the day. When the teacher pointed to a picture icon or symbol on the schedule, the students were cued in to change activities. Most importantly, the same routine was followed day in, day out.

The educators also utilized positive behavior reward systems to foster appropriate student behaviors. Positive behaviors were rewarded appropriately with praise and cheers, and, the approach to dealing with inappropriate behaviors was consistent and gentle, but firm. Teresa was sometimes stubborn and would want to do things her own way. For example, the teacher once told me that there was one time when Teresa wanted to sit in a particular chair but another child had already taken the chair. Therefore, Teresa attempted to take it by force. When the teacher stopped her, she started up a tantrum.

As a consequence, the teacher calmly walked her away from the group into "time out." Teresa was allowed to rejoin the group after she had calmed down. Because she did not like to sit away from the group, time out was an effective strategy in reducing the length of her tantrum.

This highly structured and predictable environment served Teresa well, because expectations and consequences for behavior were clearly stated and implemented consistently.

As I became familiar with the positive behavior reward system utilized in this classroom, I realized that her teachers were using the behavior modification techniques first developed decades earlier by UCLA psychologist Dr. O. Ivar Lovaas, of which I had read about in Dr. Rimland's book. The Lovaas model, which drew upon Pavlov's[2] research, was a highly structured system of rewards to encourage desirable behavior; and consequences to discourage inappropriate ones, such as the one Teresa exhibited when she wanted to take a chair from another student by force. The model depends, ultimately, upon consistency and repetition.[v]

The system can be adapted differently depending on the child, the age, and the environment (school or home); but, the basic tenets are the same: if you reward a child every time he or she shows a desired behavior, the child will most likely repeat that desired behavior, because the child will be motivated by the rewards. Conversely, if you give a child an undesired consequence following an undesired behavior, the child will most likely not repeat the undesired behavior.

Years later, when Teresa was older, I implemented an at-home positive behavior reward system to support the one in school. This was how it worked. I let her know what behavior she would be working on, like maintaining self-control (as opposed to throwing a fit) when she was denied a request. Starting at the beginning of the week, she would get a smiley face sticker any day throughout the week she demonstrated self-control following denial of a request. When she got at least 4 out of 5 stickers in the course of the week, she got treated to McDonalds on Sunday.

---

2 Ivan Pavlov was a renowned physiologist and psychologist.

At the beginning, in order to give her an opportunity to experience success and not be discouraged, I set the expectation low, with only 2 out of 5 stickers to get the reward. I then gradually increased the expectation to 3 out of 5 and eventually peaked at 4 out of 5 as her self-control ability increased.

• • •

Teresa's preschool program was individually driven, fitted to her unique needs and learning style, as required by the Individuals with Disabilities Education Act (IDEA). This special education law requires schools to provide an Individualized Education Plan (IEP) for eligible students with special needs. As a result, each child has his or her own education goals tailored to his or her individual needs.

IDEA mandates services to children with disabilities and governs how states and public agencies provide early intervention, special education, and related services to eligible infants, toddlers, children, and youths with disabilities throughout the United States. The edict was the first of its kind.[vi] Prior to its enactment in 1975, children with disabilities who were either of pre-school age (0-3 years) or of school age (3-21 years) had no national laws that protected their rights. No guidelines had addressed how and where they should be educated. In fact, many states had regulations that explicitly excluded children with certain types of disabilities from attending public schools. As a result, many of the children were left at the mercy and generosity of private and parochial schools that did what they could for them.

Some of those educated in the public schools were relegated to the basements of buildings, with staff that had no curricular training in special education. Others were confined in segregated facilities and given mediocre instruction, if any. Some children ended up in residential facilities where they were neglected under harsh conditions. Children with the most severe disabilities lived in state institutions, where they received limited or no educational or rehabilitative services.

The IDEA law changed all of that. The law, which has been revised many times over the years, ensures that children with disabilities have the opportunity to receive "Free Appropriate Public Education" (FAPE) like typical children. After its enactment, for the first time, children with disabilities had the right to be educated alongside their typical peers in the "Least Restrictive Environment" (LRE).

The law also empowers parents by making them full partners with schools in creating individualized education plans (IEPs) for their children, providing guidelines for evaluation and placement, support, related services, modification, and accommodations.

The IEP, the document that details a child's educational plans, comprises three major components. First, it describes the student's present levels and abilities (strengths and needs) in all areas affected by the disabilities; second, it states the student's educational goals and objectives aimed toward alleviating the identified areas of need; and third, it explains how the school, student, and parents should work together to meet the goals. The IEP also specifies which school or program the child will be placed into and who is responsible for implementing the goals and objectives. The plan has a lifespan of one academic year, after which it is renewed.

I am thankful that my child was born in this era when children with disabilities are given the same rights as typical children. I shudder when I think of the children born before the IDEA Law was enacted, who had to endure hardship and lack of proper education. My heart goes out to them and their families.

Teresa's IEP goal was to acquire basic communication, academic readiness, and self-help skills, the details of which illustrate the strong need at this point to help her catch up to other kids her age. At this point, she was functioning at a toddler level even though she was 4 years old. The objectives towards realizing the goal included the following:

- *She will identify, with 80% accuracy, 3 body parts by pointing when given verbal or visual cues.*
- *She will identify, with 80% accuracy, 3 articles of clothing by pointing, when verbal or visual cues are given.*
- *She will pour juice, with 80% accuracy, from a small pitcher into a cup, given physical assistance.*
- *She will use a plastic spreader, with 75% accuracy, to spread peanut butter/jelly on a cracker, given physical assistance.*
- *She will snap 4 snaps on her jacket, with 80% accuracy, given verbal cues and models.*
- *She will zip her coat, with 75% accuracy, given verbal/visual cues.*
- *When playing simple games such as peek-a-boo, she will use appropriate gestures and facial expressions with 80% accuracy.*
- *Upon hearing the word "no," Teresa will stop or withdraw from the activity with 80% accuracy.*
- *When asked to do so, she will share a toy with a peer, 4 out of 5 days per week.*
- *She will match concrete objects of up to 5 objects in each set, 80% of the time, given verbal cues.*
- *Given verbal/gesture prompts and models, she will sort objects that have large perceptual contrasts in 2 out of 3 trials.*

Teresa loved school from the first day and adjusted very well to her classroom. During the first year of preschool, her progress was remarkable, as testified to by her progress report written on April 30, 1993, about nine months after she started school. The progress was so encouraging that for the first time I held out real hope that she could learn in spite of her disability.

The report showed that she had met many of her individual educational objectives. For example, with regard to cognitive and academic readiness skills, the report indicated that she was now able to match and sort by color and shape, as well as identify several body parts.

She learned other things as well. For instance, her ability to hold a crayon or pencil and write or draw showed significant progress. She was able to imitate and copy a circle, a horizontal line, a vertical line, and a cross. She also attempted drawing a square.

Teresa's communication skills also began to emerge. She began to use one-word utterances to request objects. When she had difficulty retrieving a word, she used a mixture of jargon, gesture, and sign language to express herself; whereas before now, she pointed or held one's hand to her object of interest. She was also now able to follow many routine directions.

Progress on Teresa's social skills was no less encouraging. According to the report, her interactive skills improved. She began to initiate interactions with familiar adults by touching, establishing some eye contact, and signing or speaking. With peers, she initiated contact by touching, smiling, and establishing eye contact, albeit inconsistently. So she now interacted briefly with other kids, whereas previously, she had played by their side and ignored them. She was also now able to stay engaged and play appropriately with dolls for some time.

Regarding self-help skills, my daughter could now unfasten, unzip, unbutton, and unsnap her jackets and sweaters, although she still had some difficulty with unsnapping or unbuttoning her pants. She fed herself with a spoon and drank from a cup with little spillage.

Finally, the report noted that Teresa was able to wait her turn patiently without making a fuss. This was a big step forward!

The gains noted in my daughter's progress report did not come to me as a total surprise because I had seen great improvements at home as well. I observed that she learned and enjoyed singing her nursery rhymes, though unintelligibly. Each day, she surprised me with something new. She insisted on being able to feed herself independently, and could do so without major spilling. From the fridge, she could help herself to water, juice, milk, or snacks. She brushed her teeth independently, although I had to sing the school's teeth brushing action song to motivate her to do it.

The most impressive thing to me was her ability to troubleshoot little problems she encountered daily at play. For instance, if she was putting puzzle pieces together (and she became really good at it) and got stuck, she did not give up. She stayed with it and tried different pieces, one at a time, until she was able to eventually put all the pieces together.

As her intellect got increasingly stimulated by the school environment, I saw the emergence of a thinking being, an intelligence deep within, far beyond her outward autistic peculiarities. This made me optimistic about her future.

Teresa's preschool teacher saw something special about Teresa too: a determined spirit. She told me many times that Teresa was a very single-minded child. The teacher explained that when Teresa set her mind on doing something of great interest to her, she usually found a way to do it.

I could not agree more because I had observed that trait in her even before she started school. An example had to do with the way she was weaned off diapers. For a long time, unbeknownst to her father or me, she had watched and admired her siblings use the toilet and flushed. She was mesmerized by the action of sitting on the toilet seat and relieving oneself. But because she had no language, she said nothing. Meanwhile, I had underestimated her readiness to be weaned off diapers, so I did not even try. Even though she was almost 3 years old at the time, I thought I should give her another year before I began the "battle" of potty training because I anticipated that it was not going to be easy. I had heard stories of children with ASD who could not be toilet trained until they were in school.

Well, for us, things turned out differently. Teresa did not like the fact that she was not using the toilet like her siblings. One day, she resisted me when I tried to put on her diaper. She simply walked straight to the toilet, sat on it, used it, got up, and flushed! Then she covered her ears with both hands as she watched the flushing toilet with curiosity.

That single action of hers was my wake-up call. I stopped the diapers from then on. I used trainer panties for a few months to prevent any accidents, and after that, I switched to regular panties. She never had an accident, not even at night. I was amazed!

What this experience taught me was never to underestimate Teresa. I had assumed that because of her disability, she was not going to be ready for potty training for a long time, so I conveniently procrastinated weaning her off diapers. The child was waiting for me to do something, and when I did not, she took matters into her own hands, for good reasons.

The dramatic end to diapers was a happy coincidence for me because only a week earlier, my husband, Dele, had told me that he was tired of buying diapers and was not going to buy any more diapers for a 3-year-old child. Things were tough financially and I understood his frustration, but because I still had some supplies left, I said nothing to him. However, I was thinking of how I was going to convince him that we still needed to buy diapers. A week later, I realized I did not have to worry. My determined child had taken care of it!

Teresa's progress with preschool and the glimmers of her independent thinking were welcome beacons that helped me to realize that we could chart a course towards a decent future for my child. Some of the initial despair I had been feeling about the gravity of her ASD diagnosis began to fade and a cautious optimism took up residence in my mind and heart. The positive signs were also encouraging for Dele and our other children, bringing our family some balance and welcome normalcy on a daily basis.

# Seven

## A Huge Tantrum

## New York City
## 1993

While Teresa's progress in academic readiness and life skills was encouraging, her speech-language limitation continued to be an obstacle to significant social progress. Consequently, her public tantrums continued to be a problem.

After she had completed one year of pre-school, our family began to make plans to move to Valhalla, a small town in Westchester County, just outside New York City, where Dele was slated to continue his residency training. In preparation for the move, Teresa and I needed to travel to the County's office of special education in order to complete some paperwork. During our return trip, Teresa threw the longest fit of temper that I had seen.

Our outbound trip to Westchester County on that remarkable morning began with a subway ride from Ditmars Boulevard through Times Square to Grand Central Station. From Grand Central, we took a train heading north to Westchester County. The ride north was mostly quiet except for a pleasant, surprising act from Teresa.

Midway through our ride, she spontaneously got up and stood tall with her feet together in the middle of the aisle. Her eyes were easy and relaxed as she stared straight ahead. Then, just as spontaneously as she had gotten up, she bellowed out her ABCs up to the letter H, where she got stuck. Our co-passengers were so delighted by her action that they clapped enthusiastically. She grinned from ear to ear, obviously enjoying the applause and limelight.

One of the strangers, an elderly gentleman who was taken by her charm, afterwards tried to engage her in friendly and childlike conversation. Not surprisingly, he was unsuccessful. Teresa took one short glance at him and walked back to her seat. Then she gazed through the window, without any concern about the fuss she had started up.

Subsequently, we reached the special education office in Westchester County, took care of business in no time, and began the journey back home. Our train ride from Westchester County back to Grand Central station was uneventful. Teresa was as cool as a cucumber.

However, on arrival at Grand Central Station, she spotted a pair of escalators moving up and down. She decided she wanted to ride on them, so she attempted to pull me in that direction.

I held her firmly and redirected her toward the way leading to the shuttle that would take us to the subway trains. I explained to her that we could not go up there because that was not our way home.

As she struggled to get free of my hold, she fell to the ground crying. For a second, I considered letting her have a brief fun ride on the escalators, but I quickly decided against it because getting her off the escalators would not be easy. I would still have to deal with her resistance, so it was pointless.

While she was on the floor pitching a fit, a small crowd slowly formed around us. I could not help but feel anxiety. The crowd watched silently, trying to listen in on the dialogue between the hysterical child on the floor and me.

Seconds passed, then minutes, and my anxiety soared with every passing second. Home was still far away. How would I carry her on my shoulder all the way home? What were the onlookers thinking? Feeling pressed to explain, I told the people watching, in a shaky voice, that Teresa was a child with autism and that this type of occurrence was common with children with the condition. At hearing the word "autism," most of the people nodded their heads as if they had undergone an epiphany. Then, one by one, they slowly drifted away without saying a word.

One middle-aged man stayed behind for a moment and tried to talk Teresa out of the tantrum.

"Come on, get up and go with your mom," the kind stranger said, gently coaxing my daughter.

That caused Teresa to yell even louder.

The only reasonable option for me at that time was to wait her out. As luck would have it, after about 15 minutes she became physically spent and stopped. I took her hand gently. She offered no more resistance and quietly walked with me to take our shuttle ride to Times Square, from where we rode the N train back to Ditmars Boulevard.

Walking toward the shuttle, I heard myself promising her that when we got off the subway at Ditmars Boulevard, I would buy her favorite meal from McDonald's. That assurance comforted her, at least temporarily. Although the subway ride was quiet, it was only a lull in a long and unrelenting tantrum.

We got off the subway at Ditmars in Astoria, and went into a nearby McDonald's as promised. Teresa stood patiently with me in a long line until I bought her meal. Then, holding her hand, I turned to leave the restaurant.

We were still inside the building when Teresa let out a hair-raising shout. Convinced she was hurt, I stopped abruptly to examine her but could not find anything physically wrong. Besides, no one had come near us. I asked her what the matter was but got no response.

In a further attempt to determine the cause of her outburst, I did a quick "guess and check." Thinking perhaps she wanted to hold her bag of food, I handed it to her but that just made matters worse. She threw the bag on the floor, dropped down, and screamed even louder. I was totally perplexed. If only she could tell me what she was feeling or what her needs were.

I knew that the absence of language and, consequently, the inability to communicate her needs to me were contributing to her tantrums, but how could I manage it, pending the acquisition of language? I felt frustrated.

I thought she probably wanted to eat in the restaurant and not take the food out, so I pointed to a table and gestured for her to come with me to take our seats and eat there. She ignored my attempt and continued to cry.

Clueless as to what to try next to placate her, I picked her up onto my shoulder for our seven-block walk home. Before I could get her all the way to my shoulder, she struggled free from my hold and slipped back onto the floor where she continued to cry.

No one said a word to me, and I felt lonely, even though the restaurant was almost full to capacity. This is what parents with children living with autism live with. It is isolation deep within, born out of the feeling that people do not understand what you are going through, and even when they do, they feel it is none of their business, and so stay uninvolved. But I would say that it does matter if people approach a struggling family in the situation I just described and offer some help. I personally would have appreciated it, and think other parents in my shoes would also.

I attempted several times again to lift Teresa up, but each time she slipped right back to the floor. Finally, I managed to move her to the basement level of the restaurant, where I hoped there would be fewer people, but it turned out to be just as full as the upstairs. In any case, it was better than the upper level because, lo and behold, there was a play area for children. As soon as Teresa saw the play area, she stopped crying and ran to explore it.

Relieved at last, I sat and watched as she explored the play area with interest. After a while, I asked her if she wanted to eat her food, but she ignored me. She played alone for a long time, ignoring the other children around her. However, when I attempted a second time to walk her to our table to eat her food, she willingly followed me. We ate our food quietly and left the restaurant without any more incidents.

We had stayed in that restaurant for up to two hours. What was the reason for her tantrum at the restaurant? To this day, I have not been able to figure it out. She didn't know that there was a play area in the restaurant basement, and neither did I, so that could not have been the reason. Whatever it was, I might have known if she'd only had the language to tell me. That must have been as hard for her as it was difficult for me.

It is pertinent to mention here that the root word of *autism* is "autos," a word of Greek origin meaning "self." The term *autism* came into being over a century ago and essentially means to be isolated within the self, outside the realm of successful social interaction.[vii] When I think back on this trying day for both of us, I realize the term used to identify Teresa's daily struggles was aptly chosen.

● ● ●

Teresa's two older siblings reacted to her public tantrums in different ways. My oldest, Elohor, was understandably embarrassed by Teresa's behavior. Whenever Teresa was on my shoulders screaming as we walked the streets, Elohor preferred to keep a distance from the family so that no one would think she was part of us.

Elohor told me during one of many conversations I had with them about Teresa that she felt ashamed when other children their age stared at them. She said she was concerned that the children would look down on them for having a "weird" sister.

Ovie's reaction to the public tantrums, perhaps because he was younger, was to be outwardly sympathetic and protective of his baby sister. He did not seem embarrassed to be identified as Teresa's brother. Whenever Teresa was on the ground crying in public, he stooped beside her and tried to talk her out of her tantrums.

At times, he even took it upon himself to explain to curious onlookers what was going on. It was heartwarming to watch a 5-year-old boy try to generate sympathy for his little sister living with ASD.

Elohor's concerns made me sad, but I told her and Ovie that Teresa's behavior did not take anything away from who they were, so they both should hold their heads up high. I also told them that if people looked down on them, it was because those people were ignorant, so they should not worry about them. I reminded them that they were great kids and I was proud of them, and frequently reassured them that Teresa would eventually grow out of her tantrums. They understood and believed me.

Elohor and Ovie were very patient and cooperative. I was proud of them for the discipline and grace they exhibited when trips were either canceled or cut short because of Teresa's behavior. I could not have asked for better-behaved children.

The reaction of the public to the tantrums in New York varied. For the most part, we got stares from passersby. Many said nothing, but a few came up to me and asked what the matter was. Some even tried to talk to Teresa. I always appreciated it when strangers offered to help me when I was struggling with my children in public. In fact, one of the strangers that once helped me cross a busy street while I was wrestling with grocery bags and hanging on to my children, eventually became a good friend of mine.

The compassion of strangers was comforting for me; I felt less alone to know that people cared. When a parent is faced with all the uncertainties of raising a child with ASD, the support of one's family and community is essential to survival for both the child and the parent.

# Eight

## Westchester County, New York 1993

In the summer of 1993, our family moved to Valhalla in Westchester County, New York. We enrolled our children at the Pocantico Hills Central School (PHCS), in Tarrytown, where Teresa, then age 5, was placed in a self-contained kindergarten classroom exclusively for children with ASD and related disabilities.

Upon arrival at PHCS on the morning of her first day, Teresa leisurely emerged from the car and we walked together side by side up to her classroom, which was on the second floor of a two-story building. Despite her calm demeanor, I decided to stay with her for the entire first day because I was curious as to how her adjustment would be. After all, this was only her second school.

Her teacher, Mrs. Buck, a veteran teacher in her late forties with many years of experience, and two aides, Liz Beth and Millie, greeted us at the door. I noticed that three other students were already in the classroom playing with toys. Mrs. Buck guided Teresa to put away her jacket and lunch box, after which Teresa quickly went to help herself to some toys that she had spied on the floor. I was glad that she felt immediately comfortable in her new surroundings.

Mrs. Buck went through the day's schedule with me and asked if I had any questions. I had none but asked if I could linger for a little while. She obliged and led me to a comfortable chair in an adjacent un-used classroom. I sat near the door and waited. I was not sure what I was waiting to see or hear, but instinctively, I did not feel like leaving.

When classes began, I listened intently to all the sounds of the activi-ties taking place in Teresa's classroom for any clues as to how she was doing. I knew that I was being overprotective, but I couldn't help myself. If my presence irritated the staff, they were kind enough not to show it. I sat there for close to two hours and then dozed off.

In my sleep, I felt someone touch my shoulder. When I opened my eyes, it was the teacher, Mrs. Buck, smiling down at me, her short straight hair falling forward against her cheek.

"You may go home now," she said in a motherly tone. "She is doing just fine."

I smiled back with embarrassment and thanked her. She swished back into her classroom in her long skirt, and I went home.

At the end of the school day I returned to a jolly Teresa gripping her lunch box with one hand and waving "bye-bye" to her classmates with the other. Mrs. Buck reported that Teresa had cried on their way back from taking a walk, and she thought that she may have become fatigued under the bright sun. She assured me that when they returned to the building, Teresa had stopped crying and was given water to drink to cool off. Other than that, she told me that Teresa had a very good first day in kindergarten.

• • •

For the next two years, Teresa stayed in Mrs. Buck's classroom for kindergarten and first grade. Some of her IEP goals and objectives from the previous school were continued, and new ones were added, including: writing her name, copying the alphabet, and some pre-reading skills. She also continued to receive speech therapy.

Her kindergarten year was uneventful, but during first grade, Teresa experienced one of the most significant milestones in her education thus far: she learned the sounds of the alphabet. And I dared to hope that she would someday be able to read. Her acquisition of the alphabet sounds enabled her to decode simple, monosyllabic words like cat, man, pan, and fan, words that, in educational lingo, are called CVC (Consonant-Vowel-Consonant) patterned words.

She also learned to read a good number of sight words. Sight words are words that are not necessarily phonetically pronounced, yet are commonly found in everyday use. Examples of sight words that she recognized included: the, what, and come.

The speech therapist, Ms. Jones, integrated speech therapy with learning to read and so was partly instrumental in helping my child learn to decode words. Working one-on-one with Teresa several times a week, Ms. Jones made Teresa practice blending individual sounds to form words. She also taught her to read sight words and simple sentences.

In order to reinforce my daughter's ability to sound out words as well as maintain interest in reading, Ms. Jones created attractive but simple picture books for Teresa to read weekly. When developing the sentences for the books each week, she included the sight words that had been introduced to Teresa for that week. She also carefully selected simple words that could be decoded phonetically. She then helped Teresa practice reading the books repeatedly for up to two weeks, or until Teresa could read them independently.

The repetitive practice helped Teresa read the sentences in each book, by memorization for the most part. After that, the book was sent home for continuous practice. Another picture book was created and the same routine was repeated.

Pocantico Hills yielded other successes for Teresa, some of which carried over to the home environment. Teresa began to display more independence in the area of self-help. For example, she insisted on independently dressing herself every day and did so successfully. Not only that, she was able to tie her shoelaces perfectly, a feat that surprised me, knowing that many elementary school children still struggled with this skill. I do not know how she was taught the skill of tying shoelaces perfectly, but I do know that she learned it in Mrs. Buck's classroom. Once, when I visited the classroom, I saw a big, colorful prototype of a laced shoe in a noticeable corner in the classroom. I reckoned Teresa must have spent a lot of time there.

Other successes that transferred to the home setting included improved eye contact with family members, better appropriate play with her toys, and fewer daily tantrums.

Yet, while Teresa showed encouraging progress in the acquisition of pre-reading skills and the development of self-help, the same could not be said of speech, language, and vocabulary acquisition: progress in these areas remained slow.

It was baffling to me that she was able to decode simple words from a book and read familiar sentences from memorization, yet could not spontaneously come up with her own phrases or sentences to communicate her needs or desires. In order to express her needs, she continued to rely on pointing and gesturing, along with one-word utterances and sign language.

As I mulled over this incongruence, I realized that if language was a puzzle held in her brain, there were so many missing puzzle pieces that she could not make sense or meaning out of the bigger picture. I began to see more clearly the connection between her language deficit and her behavior. Language is the medium with which we learn and interpret the world, so when one cannot make sense out of language, one cannot understand people, situations, or events. This was my daughter's dilemma.

Her curiosity to explore the world around her increased with age, but she lacked the commensurate language ability to appropriately interpret it or interact with it. Consequently, she relied on inappropriate, primitive, or instinctive behaviors to communicate with her environment.

As a result, her behavior progressively became a series of random acts. She neither understood boundaries nor what was appropriate and inappropriate. She found it increasingly difficult to both follow directions and listen to people and was often spontaneous and unpredictable. Unfortunately, she was, for now, socially comparable to a 2-year-old toddler in the body of a first grader.

• • •

As a result of Teresa's challenging behavior pattern, sustaining a balance between caring for her and meeting the needs of my two other children became ever more daunting and sometimes had unpleasant consequences.

One example happened at the end of the school year at Pocantico Hills, when the children were getting ready for their end-of-year concerts. Elohor, who was in fourth grade, had rehearsed very hard for her role in her class performance. She was an extremely shy student and had never participated in any class performances before then. It was a big step for her to want to do this, and I was very proud of her. I could not wait to see her on stage.

We had talked about her concert role all week. She very much wanted me to see it and I promised I would. On the evening of the performances, parents, friends, and extended family members arrived at the school auditorium and took their seats with great anticipation and excitement. My three children and I arrived a little early so that Elohor and Ovie could join their classmates back stage for any last minute directions from their teachers. Teresa and I found comfortable seats at the back of the auditorium and close to the door, in the event that I needed to take her out if she became too disruptive.

No sooner did we take our seats than Teresa grew restless. She left her seat and walked around aimlessly. She touched anything or anybody within her sight, distracting the people around us. When I tried to hold her back, she physically resisted me and yelled. I tried diverting her attention toward the snacks, toys, and coloring books that I had brought for her, but they were not enough to hold her interest. It appeared as though the excitement in the air was too much for her to handle and she reacted by being hyperactive. I had no choice but to take her out of the auditorium.

When I looked at my wristwatch, I saw that there was still a good amount of time before the show started. Besides, from past experience, I recalled the fourth grade performance was usually the last one to come up. I therefore decided to dash to a nearby fast food restaurant to buy food for Teresa, something that would keep her quiet for some time. The ride to McDonald's and back was quick, just as I calculated. When we returned, I took my seat ready to enjoy the presentations, while Teresa settled down with her McDonald's meal.

Peering at the stage to fathom what was going on, I noticed that there was an intermission. It became obvious to me that the first class had just performed and exited the stage. In my mind, I was confident it could not have been fourth grade because they usually presented last. As my eyes wandered to the right side of the auditorium, I saw Elohor in the audience, walking toward the back and looking for me. She wore a relaxed smile as she walked confidently in my direction. When she reached me, she asked what I thought about her show. I looked at her bewilderedly as it slowly dawned on me that I had missed her performance by minutes. Apparently, her fourth grade class had gone against tradition and opened the show this year.

I knew she was registering the blank stare on my face. I was torn between lying and telling her the truth. I was tempted to say how fantastic the show was and how wonderfully she had performed, just like all the other parents who were praising their fourth graders around me. But I couldn't bring myself to lie to her. I had to break her heart in as gentle a way as possible. I was silent for a minute, and then I told her about Teresa's restlessness and the hurried trip I had taken to McDonald's to placate her so I could watch the performance without worrying about my youngest child bothering everyone around us.

"So you did not see me perform?" she asked, her face falling in disappointment.

I quietly nodded, at a loss for any reassuring words. How does one reassure a daughter who sang with no mother in the audience to watch? Elohor walked away with tears in her eyes and my own welled up as I watched her go back to her peers.

This incident marked a telling point in our family's journey with ASD. I knew I was the only parent in that auditorium who came but did not see her child perform.

A similar incident happened during Ovie's First Communion, on May 14, 1994. On that bright and sunny day, we drove from our apartment in Valhalla to the Holy Rosary Catholic Church, a small church located in Hawthorne, New York, not far from Valhalla. On arrival, Ovie joined his fellow communicants sitting in the first pew. Dele, Elohor, Teresa, and I sat in the middle right section of the church, and I sat at the end of our pew so I could have quick access to the aisle should there be a need to take Teresa outside. Teresa sat next to me, followed by Elohor and Dele. We waited enthusiastically for the ceremony to begin. The church was full to capacity but the congregation was pin-drop quiet.

Because we had come early, we had to wait for almost 20 minutes before the Mass started. Unfortunately, Teresa got bored easily with waiting. She started to fidget barely ten minutes after we had sat down. I gave her the snacks that I had packed for her but she was not interested. I gave her some small toys I carried in my purse, but they only held her attention for a few seconds. Soon, her fidgeting graduated to standing and walking along the pew. When I tried to hold her down, she screamed. She wanted to get to the aisle and walk around freely. If she was allowed to do that, she would touch people and run down the aisle and that would be inappropriate in the church.

Teresa was 6 years old at the time, and all the other 6-year-olds sat quietly with their parents and stared at Teresa. However, she was oblivious of their gazes. As we were trying to calm her down, Mass began. The choir sang the processional hymn and parishioners stood up to watch the procession of priests, liturgical ministers, and Mass servers make their way to the altar. The scene got Teresa intrigued, so she stood on her seat and started to make loud noises of excitement. She stared at everyone around her and started to laugh with apparent jubilation. Her noise level increased with every passing minute and people were beginning to look at us as if to say, "Aren't you going to do something?"

At that point, we knew it was time to remove her from the church. Dele took her outside, and they stayed out for the entire duration of the service, including the First Communion ceremony. At the beginning of the actual ceremony, Ovie and his fellow recipients filed to the back of the church. From there, each child was flanked by his mom on his left and dad on his right, and all three took a slow, nervous walk to the front of the church where the child received his or her very First Communion. Ovie, whose last name began with a Z, was the last one to walk because the communicants were lined up in alphabetical order. During our walk, I stood on his left side, without his dad on his right side, and walked him to receive his very First Communion. Of the dozen or more boys and girls that took communion that day, my son was the only one without his father by his side.

There were many moments such as these, where our parental desires to support our two older children in some important way were compromised by Teresa's louder needs for special attention to maintain appropriate behavior in public settings. It was heartbreaking, but at the same time, it was an unavoidable aspect of family life with a member of the fold having ASD. On the one hand, we all understood and worked together. On the other hand, we wished for normalcy at times, and wished for the language key to unlock the communication barriers that typified our daily struggles with Teresa's behavior.

# Nine

## St. Louis, Missouri
## 1995

One day during her first year in an inclusive classroom, Teresa brought home information about a class project. It was an integrated science research project where students were required to research a wild animal of their choice. For the presentation piece, they needed to write short factual notes about the animal, make a poster of the animal, and present their report to the class.

Teresa was now in a second-grade inclusive classroom at the Wren Hollow Elementary School in the Parkway School District in St. Louis, Missouri. We had moved to St. Louis in the summer of 1995, after Dele completed his residency training at Valhalla, New York.

Broadly defined, an inclusive classroom is one where children with disabilities are educated alongside typically developing students in a regular classroom, while an aide or special educator provides appropriate accommodations and support. In her previous schools, Teresa had been placed in self-contained classrooms where all the children had autism or related disabilities. So this was a very different educational setting for Teresa.

After Dele and I read the integrated science research project information, we looked at each other thinking, *they do not expect her to do this,
do they?*

Well, they did—with a great deal of modification and support.
Throughout the process, her general education teacher and aide were
flexible and allowed Teresa to participate to any degree that she could.
With the guidance of the special education aide, Teresa selected the jaguar by pointing to a picture of a jaguar from a book of animals. The aide
researched the basic facts about jaguars and wrote them on three index
cards, in very simple, short sentences amenable to memorization. Each
note card had three sentences and looked something like this:

*Note card 1*
*The jaguar is a member of the cat family.*
*It is a mammal because it feeds its young with milk.*
*Its habitat is the forest.*

*Note card 2*
*It eats smaller animals.*
*Its color is orange and black.*
*It is the largest cat in America.*

While her peers were expected to write lengthy notes on multiple note
cards and provide numerous details about their animals, the expectation for Teresa was to have only three note cards written by her aide. It
was a developmentally appropriate modification.

The aide made two sets of the note cards. One set was sent home
for home practice and the other was left in school for school practice.
Teresa had three weeks to learn the facts on the note cards and prepare
her poster.

When I saw the note cards, I was skeptical; I didn't think I could
encourage her to even look at the note cards, let alone get her to read
and memorize them. But what I did not count on was the power of her

ability for rote memorization, a skill she'd developed at Pocantico Hill Elementary School, when her speech therapist frequently created picture books that she read by memorization.

What surprised me even more was that she was actually interested in the note cards. One motivation was that she liked animals, and I also suspected that she wanted to do what her classmates in school were doing. She might have intuited that the note cards were something expected of everybody and she wanted to be part of that.

Teresa and I started reading the note cards every day after dinner, and each time, to my surprise, she cooperated well. We would huddle side by side at the dining room table while her siblings were upstairs in their rooms also doing homework. The TV in the living room droned in the background where my husband was unwinding after a non-stop day at the clinic. I would hold up a card and Teresa, swinging her bare feet as she sat, would tackle them word-by-word. Her expression was surprisingly relaxed as she concentrated. Occasionally she would smile.

"Good job," I kept interjecting at key points during our sessions, which would trigger her smile.

We worked on the first two sentences during the first few days, and I encouraged her to repeat the sentences over and over again, without looking at the note card. When she had successfully memorized the first two sentences on note card 1, I became confident that she could memorize the rest. We continued to work on two sentences at a time until she was able to memorize all the sentences on all three of the note cards. Although her articulation of the words was poor and sometimes hard to discern, I was greatly encouraged by this small success.

According to her aide, on the day of the oral presentations, the students took turns reading their reports to the class while the teacher videotaped them. When it was Teresa's turn, she was initially hesitant and did not get up immediately when asked. However, when the aide took her hand, she went willingly past the grouped desks, where her peers were sitting and watching, to the front of the room where the teacher was waiting with the camera. Her aide stood by her side to prompt her whenever necessary.

With her eager and supportive classmates ready to cheer, Teresa stood in front of the classroom, note cards in hand, and began to say her facts. Head down, she spoke hesitantly and incoherently, but she spoke the words:

"The jaguar is a member of the cat family. It is a mammal because it feeds its young with milk."

After the first two sentences, she stopped, continuing to look downward. Perhaps she had forgotten what to say due to nervousness. Her peers smiled encouragingly, but stayed quiet to give her time to speak.

"It's okay. You're doing great!" Her aide whispered and then gestured for Teresa to go ahead and look at her cards.

Almost inaudibly, and with some hesitation, she read all the sentences on the note cards. When she finished, her classmates cheered. Some students even got up and gave her a spontaneous hug. Teresa was all smiles.

To her admiring audience, it didn't matter that she had her head down for most of the duration and hardly made eye contact with anyone. It didn't matter that her articulation of the words was poor and difficult to understand. As far as they were concerned, her presentation was a success. Her aide told me how proud she was of Teresa in that moment; she was, in fact, elated.

The joy and celebration around the classroom was infectious. The aide held up Teresa's jaguar poster for everyone to see. It was a big, yellow, clearly drawn cat with brown spots that Teresa had created with the aide's assistance. The class stood and clapped while she smiled shyly. The imperfection of her end product was irrelevant, because her experience through the entire process was priceless.

As I witnessed her success, I learned never to assume my daughter could not do what her classmates were doing. From that day on, I encouraged her to try anything her peers were asked to do, even when it looked impossible. Because she learned better by imitating their actions,

I advocated for and sought out opportunities inside and outside of school to integrate her with all kinds of children her age.

My daughter's success in the inclusive classroom was also due to the positive attitude of Mrs. Helen Morrison, her regular education teacher. From the first day, she received Teresa with open arms. Under her kind and professional tutelage, my child was a full participant in most classroom activities, in spite of her severe speech impairment and poor behavior.

Even though Teresa did not fully understand many of the things that were done in the inclusive classroom, she was given a chance to experience by watching and participating. The staff communicated with Teresa through a combination of speech, sign language, symbols, and picture exchange.

One might assume that because of Teresa's disability, she would be unlikely to excel in any area in the inclusive classroom. But she proved that to be false when she showcased her unique talent for penmanship.

Though cursive handwriting was taught, no one predicted that my child would not only acquire the skill, but would run away with it within a short time. She mastered the art of cursive handwriting so well, and impressed Mrs. Morrison so much, that Mrs. Morrison took a sample of Teresa's cursive handwriting to many classrooms in the school to show other teachers and students what Teresa could do in penmanship. None of her peers wrote in cursive as well as Teresa did. In fact, Mrs. Morrison shared with me that Teresa's cursive handwriting was better than any that she had seen in her many years of teaching. Everyone in school came to know my daughter as the cursive handwriting expert of the second grade. What a surprising gift!

The best part of Teresa's inclusive experience had to do with the way her enthusiastic classmates befriended and accepted her just the way she was. They came to know and understand her as a person, and fondly guided her throughout the day. In fact, they fussed over who would be her buddy on any given day. There was so much interest in being her guide or pal that the teacher had to place all the students on a schedule, so that they took turns to be her buddy.

The buddy walked with Teresa during transitions to lunch, the bathroom, music class, physical education class, and any other place that the class needed to go. One of her buddies became so over-protective that on one particular day, freedom-loving Teresa resisted by running away from her buddy during a transition. Her frantically worried buddy ran back to the classroom to report to Mrs. Morrison that Teresa had run off, and my little runaway threw the whole school into frenzy. For a few minutes, there was a desperate search of the building by the principal, his assistant, and the office staff, all armed with walkie-talkies. The search finally ended when Teresa was found in an isolated part of the building, contentedly playing. Everyone sighed with relief.

When Teresa was not running away from her attentive buddies, they stayed by her side and gave her support in music and physical education classes. Because of her strong desire to do what her peers did, she keenly watched and imitated them during instruction. In time, she could imitate actions in music class so well that she got weaned off buddy support. The use of a buddy during transition to and from music class was also phased out because she was now able to walk to class responsibly. Thus music class became the first inclusive classroom where Teresa displayed total independence. It was also there that her love for music was ignited.

● ● ●

During 2nd grade, Teresa spent half of her time in the inclusive classroom and the other half in a special education resource room where the special education teacher provided instruction on basic academic skills in reading, writing, math, and addressed her IEP objectives in either a small group or a one-on-one basis.

Mrs. Wade was Teresa's special education teacher. In addition to the classroom instruction and support that she gave Teresa and her peers, Mrs. Wade also planned many community-based learning experiences where the children had opportunities to transfer the skills they were learning in the classroom to a community setting. For instance, the children learned to identify coins by name in class and then demonstrated the use of money by going out to local garage sales to buy small items. Teresa loved the garage sale trips and brought home toys and jewelry that caught her fancy, which she paid for with her pocket money.

Slowly and methodically, through specific learning strategies and interventions, as well as reinforcements at home, Teresa's world was expanding as she made friends, interacted with the community, and learned appropriate behaviors from supportive peer role models.

# Ten

## St. Louis, Missouri
## 1997

At home, Teresa and I enjoyed our time together. She particularly enjoyed our bedtime "read aloud." She also loved to ride her bike, with me tagging alongside. I could tell that she was having fun from her loud laughter and happy face as she pedaled down the street in her leggings, ponytail bouncing.

Yet, in all the time we spent together as mother and daughter, she did not show any outward affection, such as initiating hugs, like typical children do. When I hugged her, she neither resisted nor hugged back, maintaining neutrality instead. This was why I never forgot the day she demonstrated her compassionate side for the first time.

It was the day I heard that my father had passed away. I woke up on the morning of February 4, 1997 and went about my daily chores. It was just another day. I was in the kitchen preparing breakfast when Dele came to me and invited me to sit down with him at the dining table. Instinctively, I knew something was wrong because my husband never invited me to sit down before he told me anything, and I could not imagine what could be wrong.

*It can't be anything to do with the children,* I thought, *because they are all here at home playing.* As I followed him to the table, I wondered what it could be.

When I sat down, he told me solemnly that my sister had called from Nigeria the previous night and broken the news that my father had passed away peacefully in his sleep in his hospital bed, while recovering from a minor surgery. I broke down crying uncontrollably, the news of my dad's sudden death flooding me with grief. He was gone. In my haze of profound sadness, I couldn't imagine that I would ever have the impulse to laugh again. I went into our bedroom and collapsed at the foot of the bed wailing, which awakened Teresa, who was sleeping on our bed.

When she opened her eyes and saw me crying, she reached out to me and hugged me.

"What's wrong, mommy, what's wrong?" she said.

"Mommy does not feel good," I managed to respond.

I simply kept on crying, not sure how to explain the concept of death to her, or even able to stop crying long enough to do so. At that moment, all she needed to know was that I didn't feel good. She hugged me tighter and we hugged each other for a while in silence. Then she suddenly broke the hug.

"No school today?" she asked hopefully.

"No school today," I replied, and couldn't help but smile.

Obviously thrilled at the prospect of not going to school, she grinned and quickly laid back in bed (before I changed my mind), pulled her blanket over her tiny body, and went back to sleep. I found her reaction amusing, although I could not laugh at the time. But I knew, at that moment, that as long as I had Teresa, I would laugh again.

Our exchange was remarkable not only because she hugged me, but also because it marked the first time that Teresa communicated using a phrase and a complete sentence in meaningful context. This language breakthrough and her first spontaneous hug for me tempered my sadness—a splash of sunshine that lit up a dark and dreary day.

# Eleven

## St. Louis, Missouri
## 1996

At the end of 2nd grade at Wren Hollow Elementary School, Teresa's IEP team met to review her progress and create new goals for the following school year. The team consisted of all the required members: the special education teacher, a regular education teacher, an administrator, the school psychologist, and me.

At the meeting, Teresa's progress was determined to be satisfactory because she had met most of her annual goals and objectives. The ones that were not met would be carried over to the following year, and the team would develop additional goals and objectives.

In discussing classroom placement, the regular education teacher informed us that the third grade class was going to be a lot more challenging than second grade had been. For example, the concepts of division and multiplication would be introduced in math, and they usually posed a great challenge for students. Teresa would have to master addition and subtraction with regrouping (or carrying) in order to understand the concepts of multiplication and division. It was noted that Teresa had not yet mastered addition and subtraction with regrouping.

Furthermore, while her basic phonetic reading skills continued to improve, she was still not a reader, per se. The team also observed that she was still socially immature and her speech remained severely inadequate. Based on this information, the team decided to retain Teresa in second grade, in spite of progress on her individual goals.

The team agreed that an additional year in second grade would give her the opportunity to not only work on basic skills, but also grow in the other deficient areas. I agreed with the decision because it was in her best interest.

Her retention in second grade proved extremely beneficial for Teresa's learning readiness. She developed even more significantly, which put her in a much better position to engage in third grade curriculum the following year.

It was also during this time that the cover of books opened for my daughter in a meaningful way. While her teachers intensified reading instruction at school, I was trying new strategies at home. Little did we know that our combined efforts were about to unlock Teresa's potential to become a bona fide oral reader. During this year, Teresa made the leap from rote memorization of familiar texts to phonetically and consistently decoding unfamiliar words. As a result, her interest and motivation for reading soared, which took all of us by surprise.

For my part at home, I bought the Scholastic Phonics Reading Series, which was comprised of little phonics books with levels from one to twenty. The first level involved simply reading the alphabet, but subsequent levels gradually shifted from reading the alphabet to reading words and, ultimately, sentences.

Each night at bedtime, instead of me reading a story to her, Teresa and I read the phonics books together, starting with the first level and working our way up. At first I took the lead, doing most of the reading as she struggled to blend individual sounds to make words. As time went by, she was able to blend sounds into words more accurately, consistently, and confidently; so, I gradually released my lead role to her and supported her on the side. Over time, she reached a point where she was able to read the entire series easily without any support. Surprised by her own ability to read well, she could not get enough of reading and enthusiastically read the series over and over to me at bedtime.

Teresa's determination and tenacity for reading astonished me because she normally had difficulty focusing and attending to anything. Yet, here she was able to sustain focus on the little phonics books during our bedtime reading sessions. I concluded again that Teresa's driving force came from watching her typical peers read and wanting to be like them.

At school, Mrs. Wade, her special education teacher, was just as pleasantly surprised at Teresa's reading progress as I was. She had noticed that Teresa was beginning to read books independently in class. One day she sent home a note asking what I was doing with Teresa at home. I asked Mrs. Wade the same question, informing her that I had also witnessed tremendous improvement in Teresa's reading. I wanted to know what she was doing in school! Mrs. Wade explained that she was using the EdMark Reading Program as a supplement to her reading instruction, and I told her about the Scholastic Phonics Reading Series that I used at home. Apparently, each of us, unbeknownst to the other, had found an effective tool to help Teresa learn to read, tools which worked well in tandem, reinforcing just the right skills and approach.

After Teresa gained fluency in reading the Scholastic series, she took the books to school and would not let them out of her sight. Because Teresa liked the books so much, Mrs. Wade decided to incorporate the books in her behavior management plan by using them as incentives for completing school work; such that, if Teresa completed her work in class, she would be given free time to go to a corner and read the series.

The positive reinforcement plan paid off because Mrs. Wade got much more class work from Teresa than she had gotten previously. In a note to me, Mrs. Wade said that Teresa made it clear in no uncertain terms that she wanted the books to go home in her backpack each day!

The fact that Teresa could decode words and read phonetically gave me the impetus to push her to acquire more vocabulary. I reasoned that if she could amass a sizable bank of words, she might be more inclined to use them in speech. I determined that she was not talking much because she did not have a wealth of vocabulary upon which to draw.

Consequently, I decided to teach her new vocabulary, one word at a time. Initially, I focused on helping her learn the names of objects around the house. Every day, for about five or ten minutes, I lined up five objects in front of her—a variety of household things such as a hairbrush, a spoon, a sock, a book, and an orange. I named one object aloud at a time and guided her to point to that object. After that, I pointed to the object and asked her to name it aloud.

I stayed with the same five objects every day until she gained mastery of them. Then I introduced five new objects and repeated the steps. She enjoyed this activity, thinking it was a game, while unconsciously mastering the names of many household items.

During the year she repeated second grade, Teresa also demonstrated a keen ability to spell words with more intricate patterns than the basic Consonant-Vowel-Consonant (CVC) pattern. Her second grade spelling words comprised a variety of word patterns including the short vowel sounds found in words like *flat, last, went, rest, spot, drop, but,* and *bugs.* Other words included the long vowel sounds such as *line* and *mine,* as well as *home* and *coat.* The second grade list also contained words with "r-controlled vowels" like *start, card, shirt, bird,* and *mother,* in addition to words with the "-ing" ending like *doing, running,* and *looking.*

Her teacher gave weekly spelling tests, and on her first spelling test Teresa spelled an impressive 90% of the words correctly. The following week, she scored 100%. This trend continued throughout her stay at Wren Hollow.

Teresa's arithmetic skills also improved. She learned to add and subtract single-digit numbers using counters and began to learn to do addition of double-digit numbers, with and without regrouping (carrying). She did so well with math facts in her inclusive classroom that she became one of a few members of an "exclusive club" of students who often received ice cream sundaes as a reward for scoring 100% on weekly math fact tests.

My daughter acquired a lot more than math facts in math. In the resource room with Mrs. Wade, she learned to identify coins by name and to use a calculator to add numbers. She also learned how to use a calendar to record events of interest like birthdays, as well as how to tell time to the hour. She checked Mrs. Wade's wristwatch numerous times during the day and knew exactly when it was lunchtime, her favorite time of the day.

It was also during this time that we discovered Teresa's artistic creativity and love for drawing, coloring, and decorating. In art class, her drawings were comprised mostly of hearts, rainbows, and the sun—three of her favorite things. When students were asked to draw a particular object, Teresa always found a spot to include her hearts, a rainbow, and the sun. It was very easy to pick out her art from a display of student work because all you needed to do was look for those three things, which constantly appeared together, always beautifully drawn and colored.

Teresa's ability to use spontaneous language in the proper context also thankfully began to emerge during this school year. One day, out of the blue, she told Mrs. Wade that her birthday was in April and then blurted out many different numbers. The numbers 2 and 6 were among the last numbers she mentioned. Mrs. Wade looked up Teresa's birthday for verification and found out it was April 26. This incident excited Mrs. Wade because, even though Teresa could read words out of the pages of a book, she did not yet have an array of independent speech. It thus marked another rare instance when Teresa's utterance was spontaneous and functional.

When Mrs. Wade told me that Teresa had vocalized the correct month and day of her birthday, I was overjoyed. It was a mark of progress, and therefore cause for celebration. I praised Teresa when she came home from school and danced my Nigerian victory dance in front of her. Clueless as to why I was celebrating, my daughter looked at me fleetingly and walked away. My amateur dance steps, on the other hand, were of great amusement to Elohor and Ovie.

At another time, Mrs. Wade heard Teresa using words in a meaning-ful context and she shared this success with me in her daily note home:

*Mrs. Zoma,*

*Teresa said to me, "Be right back" (something I'm always saying in-termittently during the day to her, when I come and go); however, this was the first time I heard her say it at an appropriate time. She was leaving with one of the girls to go to the library.*

*Also, she carried on what was close to a conversation, a discussion about Clayton's book (a Pooh book), which he had brought from home and that she admired and wanted to take home.*

*She used single words but definitely got her point across. Very good; more words all together than we heard before. She talked me into allow-ing her to take Clayton's book home. Please return the book. I made her promise to return the book.*

*Mrs. Wade*

*Special education teacher*

Mrs. Wade's observation was right on target, as I had also witnessed one incident at home when Teresa used a word in the right context. She had accidentally locked herself in the bathroom and could not get out. I do not know how long she was there, but I heard a loud voice coming from upstairs bellowing out "HELP!" It was Teresa's voice!

I could not ascertain exactly where she was yelling from, so I made my way upstairs and discovered she was locked in the bathroom. I opened the door and gave her a much needed hug.

"Good job for saying help!" I said.

She was not as thrilled as I was. She just ran off, happy to be free again.

# Twelve

## St. Louis, Missouri
## 1996

**E**ncouragingly, Teresa had begun using some spontaneous contextually appropriate language, but her overall speech was still grossly deficient. The speech and language domain was one important area where she did not show any significant progress despite weekly speech therapy, the opportunity to socialize with typical peers, and ample exposure to stimulating educational environments both in school and at home. I could not understand why she was not improving and felt frustrated.

Standardized testing conducted in April 1996 indicated that at 8 years old, Teresa was operating below 2 years and 11 months old in both receptive and expressive language. During her initial evaluation at age 4 in New York, her Receptive Communication Age (RCA) and Expressive Communication Age (ECA) were determined to be 12 months old.

If the two evaluations were juxtaposed, they would reveal that in a span of four years Teresa had made only roughly 23 months' gain in receptive and expressive language, despite speech therapy and many other educational interventions.

Her preferred mode of communication still consisted mostly of holding my hand and pointing me to her object of interest, or using gestures. Even though she had acquired more vocabulary words, Teresa did not use them spontaneously to communicate; she always had to be cued or prompted to use them. On the rare occasions when she spoke, her speech was mostly telegraphic in nature, consisting of short phrases. For example, she said, "cookie, please" when her intention was to say, "May I have some cookies, please?" Also, signs of echolalia (parrot-like repetition) still remained in her speech.

During this time, I would have been happy if she had used telegraphic speech consistently to communicate, but she did not. It took considerable effort to prompt her to speak using a phrase or a simple short sentence. In school, teachers continued to rely on sign language, picture exchange, and symbols to communicate with her. At home, I used a combination of speech and a few signs that I knew, like "yes," "no," "more," and "finish" to express myself to her. She expressed herself using one word utterances, sign language, and pointing.

Her socialization skills also developed at a snail's pace. This was not surprising because social skills often develop hand-in-hand with speech and language. Her interaction and socialization with her classmates was most often encouraged or orchestrated by her teacher rather than occurring spontaneously. Her desire to voluntarily hang out or play with her peers did not progress. She preferred to play alone. Teresa liked to be in their midst as an observer of their actions but not as a participant. She did not appear to comprehend a lot of what they said and tried to get away from them when she found their friendly moves overwhelming.

Furthermore, my daughter was still unable to make social decisions on her own and always looked to adults for help whenever a peer was treating her unfairly. Mrs. Wade shared with me her concern that Teresa neither had the language skill nor the awareness to defend herself from her peers when the situation warranted it. She continued to be immature for her age.

With regard to her behavior, there were still challenges, although huge tantrums such as the ones seen in New York no longer occurred. Teresa still had difficulty following directions, focusing, and paying attention. She was easily distracted and displayed off-task behaviors in class. Sometimes, she did not complete her assignments. She was almost completely unaware of social improprieties and consequently engaged in giggles and silliness at inappropriate times.

The special education teacher utilized a behavior management system to encourage appropriate behavior in school. The system incorporated a variety of incentives and positive reinforcements one of which was free time to spend with a certain student of whom Teresa was fond. Paul was a child with Fragile X syndrome and the two kids really enjoyed spending time together. At the end of each morning session (before lunchtime), Teresa was given free time to be with Paul if she completed her work. Paul's picture was taped to her desk as a reminder of what she had to look forward to. The teacher reported that Teresa's speed and work completion rate increased as a result of this incentive. But overall, behavior remained poor.

At home, Teresa did not throw any more huge tantrums; although she was inflexible in her ways and made a fuss when things were either out of routine or did not go her way. Also, her lack of understanding of social norms caused us to stay home more often than we wished. She was still sometimes rough in her ways; for instance, in public, she shoved strangers who were in her way and took people's things without asking. At age 8, she was tall for her age, so it was hard for people to understand why a child this big was behaving so immaturely.

As I thought about Teresa's prognosis, I remained focused on my ultimate wish for her: I wanted her to grow up to be the best that she could be, to reach her full potential, whatever that might be. This meant that I had to ensure that she had access to every available, viable educational opportunity. She was making progress academically and I expected that to continue. She had acquired interests and skills in music and art, skills she could use for leisure and enjoyment.

However, her communication, behavior and social immaturity remained major obstacles to her progress. It is hard to achieve a successful life without adequate communication abilities and appropriate social interaction with others.

At home, I tried to manage behavior by using positive reinforcements such as snacks, praise, and "high fives" to encourage appropriate behavior but my efforts met with little success. So far, the school interventions and home strategies alone had not manifested the essential growth my child needed. At this juncture, I was resolved to seek alternative ways to work on communication, behavior, and social skills. I wanted to explore the possibility of medical treatment.

I had many questions. Was it really true that there is no cure for autism? What about treatment? Were there physicians that specialize in autism? If so, where could I find such physicians? Were there medications that could remedy Teresa's atypical behaviors and improve her speech? How could I keep abreast of all the latest research, treatment options, and programs for autism? What if I were missing out on some beneficial therapies or medicines that were already out there? How could I find out all that there was to know about autism? I knew a lot of research was going on in the field but did not know how to access points of contact. I wanted a physician who was an autism expert who would tell me the current available data and research.

Daily, these questions weighed heavily on my mind, creating pressure and stress. I felt like time was running out. My desire for my daughter to reach her full potential kicked an intensive search phase into high gear.

# Thirteen

## More Tests

## St. Louis, Missouri
## 1997

My search for an autism expert led me to Dr. Philip Light, a popular child neurologist who had made his mark in the St. Louis community. He frequently gave talks about autism to parents, professionals, and care providers. It was during one of these talks that I met Dr. Light for the first time. At the conclusion of his talk, I introduced myself as a parent having a child with autism. He gave me his business card and the very next day I called his office to set up an appointment.

Teresa and I had an initial consultation with Dr. Light in January 1997. During our visit, I told him my concerns and fears regarding Teresa's insufficient social development and communication skills. I elaborated on her attention difficulties, inappropriate public behaviors, her lack of functional language, and her social immaturity. I told him that I was worried because at age 8 these atypical behaviors were impediments to learning and if not remedied now, they could pose significant challenges for Teresa in the future. I expressed my desire to learn about current research, and shared my curiosity about any medications that could treat Teresa's autistic symptoms.

Dr. Light listened attentively with apparent empathy. Then, he asked me a range of questions regarding my pregnancy with Teresa, her birth, her early development, and her academic progress in school. He also inquired about our family's medical and psychological history. He then did a physical examination of Teresa, as well as a clinical observation of her interaction with me.

During the examination, Teresa was alert. At one point while the doctor was observing her, she twirled around on the doctor's swivel stool muttering words she had heard from a Dr. Seuss tape. When the doctor engaged her in conversation, she followed his directions and did as she was told.

The doctor asked her to point to her body parts as he named them one at a time. She was able to correctly identify her eye, nose, mouth, ears, head, hand, and leg. On request by Dr. Light, Teresa recited her ABCs to Z and counted to 100. She was given paper and pencil to copy some shapes and write her name, both of which she did successfully.

At the end of our visit, Dr. Light briefly shared his opinion with me, and about a week later he mailed his full report. According to his report, he found Teresa to be "well developed, well-nourished, and in no distress." He pointed out that her extremities were "normal and neurological examination showed a normal skull and spine." He described her gait as normal and reported that her "cranial nerve examination was normal." The doctor found "no tremor, drift, or involuntary movement," and she had normal muscle tone. He noted that she was "ultrasensitive to tactile stimuli, especially around the face and head."

His overall impression was that Teresa had "minimal cerebral dysfunction, manifested by atypical pervasive developmental disorder." In other words, Teresa had a mild impairment in her brain, and her current underdeveloped behaviors were evidence of that. From Dr. Light's report, it was also evident that the various parts of Teresa's physical brain appeared to be relatively normal, yet her development of cognitive functioning was atypical and far-reaching. He recommended the following tests:

- *EEG awake and asleep*
- *serum lead urine amino acid screen*
- *DNA analysis/check chromosomes for Fragile X*

The doctor explained each test that my child was going to take. Since there is an association between seizures and autistic and language problems, he recommended the electroencephalogram (EEG) to be used to track Teresa's brain activity to see if there was any evidence of seizures. He said that statistics show that epilepsy (seizures of unknown cause) is prevalent among 20 to 40 percent of people with autism spectrum disorders, and the highest rates are found among those with the most severe forms of autism. The test would therefore eliminate the possibility that seizures were playing a role in Teresa's disability.

The urine amino acid screen is done to detect any abnormalities in amino acid content. Amino acids are components of all of the body's proteins, and, any abnormality in the metabolism of amino acids may lead to intellectual development disorders or other problems. In some of the amino acid disorders, treatment may help to prevent or address intellectual disorders.

The Fragile X chromosome test is done to determine if a child has a genetic condition involving changes in part of the X chromosome. The symptoms of Fragile X are similar to those of autism spectrum disorder, and it is because of this behavioral similarity with autism that the Fragile X chromosome test is ordered.

According to Dr. Light, some symptoms of Fragile X syndrome that are similar to those of autism include the following:

- *Hand clapping or hand biting*
- *Hyperactive or impulsive behavior*
- *Intellectual development disorder*
- *Speech and language delay*
- *Tendency to avoid eye contact*

In April 1997, three months after our initial visit, we had a follow-up visit with Dr. Light to review the test results. He reported that Teresa had a normal serum lead urine amino acid screen, ruling out amino acid abnormality as a root cause of her symptoms. The DNA test showed normal chromosomes, ruling out Fragile X syndrome. He informed me that the result of the EEG (which was done in an "awake state" in the doctor's office) was inconclusive. Excessive movements of the head, body, eyes, or tongue, and, the inability to remain still throughout the test, can interfere with the accuracy of an EEG.

Teresa had difficulty meeting these standards during the awake test as she failed to cooperate with the doctor's instructions and continued to wiggle and move during the test. So, Dr. Light ordered another EEG test. This time it would be an overnight recording during a "sleep state" at a hospital. We were scheduled to check into the St. Louis Children's Hospital less than a week later for the second EEG.

The doctor gave me a paper containing standard guidelines to follow for the days leading up to the test. The guidelines advised against giving Teresa any form of medications, such as sedatives and tranquilizers, sleep medications, or medicines used to treat seizures. The presence of these medications would affect the brain's usual electrical activity and produce abnormal test results. Teresa was not taking any such medications, so the directive was not applicable to us. She was also to avoid certain foods that contained caffeine, such as tea, cola, and chocolate for at least 8 hours before the test. In addition, she was expected to eat a small meal shortly before the test, as low blood sugar could produce abnormal test results. Because electrodes would be attached to Teresa's scalp, it was important that her hair was clean and free of grease, sprays, oils, creams, lotions, or other hair products. To that effect, I shampooed her hair the evening before we went into the hospital.

In order to detect certain types of abnormal electrical activity in the brain, Teresa would need to be asleep during the recording. By the advice of the doctor, therefore, I reduced her normal sleep time considerably the night before the test day so that she would be very tired by the time we arrived at the hospital. I kept her busy at play until close to midnight when I finally allowed her to go to bed. She woke up around 6:30 a.m., but I kept her from taking naps throughout the day. At 4 p.m. we left for the hospital.

We arrived at the St. Louis Children's Hospital at around 4:30 p.m. After completing the necessary paperwork, we were led by an EEG technician to an EEG preparation room. An elevated bed occupied the center of the room.

Teresa was asked to lie on her back with her eyes closed in preparation for setting electrodes on her head. It was hard to keep her stable because she kept opening her eyes and giggling in anticipation of what the technician was going to do to her. The technician proceeded to attach what looked like small, flat, metal discs to different parts of Teresa's scalp, using a sticky white paste to hold the electrodes in place.

It was a long and painstaking procedure; for one electrode to be attached, a section of her long, tangled hair had to be parted in order to access her scalp. Parting her tight curly hair was painful, so Teresa was predictably uncooperative. She constantly attempted to remove the technician's hands from her hair. Soon, her giggles of excitement were replaced by vehement wails of protest.

Sometimes, electrodes that had already been attached slipped out of position and had to be re-attached. Luckily, the technician was patient and gentle, yet firm and persistent. Despite Teresa's vocal and physical resistance, the technician was eventually able to attach all the electrodes successfully.

After the preparation, Teresa was moved to her ward for the night. Once she was there, the technician connected the electrodes via wires to a speaker and recording machine. It was odd to watch the electrical activity in my daughter's brain migrating across a computer screen in wavy lines.

During the recording, Teresa was expected to stay in bed without moving until she naturally fell asleep. Waiting for Teresa to fall asleep was one of the longest moments of my life. I sat on a chair by her side the whole time and watched her fidget, turn, twist, giggle, and laugh with excitement. She wanted to sit up and look out the window.

For the first hour or so she thought it was really cool to be in this strange bed and strange room with a view. She found the whole experience pleasurable and laughed uncontrollably sometimes. Soon after, she became bored, especially when it became clear to her that she was not going to be allowed to leave the bed and roam around freely.

I did not want the test to be compromised this time around and feared the electrodes on her head might slip off, so I kept holding her down whenever she wanted to leave the bed to roam. Being a naturally hyperactive child, it was hard for Teresa to lie still in bed for hours without any form of entertainment to keep her occupied. After what seemed like eternity, she fell asleep around 10 p.m., although she woke up off and on during the night because of the discomfort of the electrodes. I also had to call the nurse when she needed to use the restroom, at which time the recording was temporarily stopped.

The next morning, after a long night, the electrodes were removed from Teresa's head and we were discharged from the hospital. I was told that our doctor would get back to us with the result in about a week. On our way home, I praised Teresa for going through with the difficult test; and, though I was exhausted, we stopped for a special treat of hamburgers and fries at McDonald's.

When we arrived home, I tried to shampoo Teresa's hair. The white paste used to glue the electrodes was not easy to remove. Despite multiple shampoos, a lot of the whitish substance still floated throughout her hair like snowflakes. Ultimately, I had no choice but to cut her beautiful long hair. When I reluctantly approached her with the scissors, her face merely showed curiosity as to what I was doing. As I began to cut, she sat very still and did not resist. While I worked, I explained the reason we had to cut her hair. She said nothing but smiled. I cut it to about an inch in length all over until it looked like a short Afro style. Contrary to my expectation, and to my relief, Teresa liked her short cut and never again wanted to grow her hair long. From then on, whenever her hair grew long and when combing became painful because of the kinky nature of her hair, she would ask for a haircut. Thankfully, the daily struggle I experienced in getting her cooperation to comb her curly, long hair was now history!

A week later, we visited Dr. Light. He reported that no seizures were detected in the EEG. That was good news. I was really not surprised by the results because I had never observed any seizures in my child, so I was simply happy to have the rigors of the tests out of the way so we could move forward to discuss effective treatment for autism.

With all the tests out of the way, our discussion shifted to treatment options. I asked Dr. Light about medication options to treat autism and the behaviors Teresa exhibited. First, he emphasized that there was indeed no cure for autism. Then, he told me that there was no single medication that could treat autism, although individual symptoms could be treated. For example, symptoms of attention deficit and hyperactivity disorder, ADHD (difficulty with focusing, paying attention, staying on task, etc.), could be treated with medication.

He further explained that there were some medicines traditionally used for patients with ADHD that had been tried on children with autism to address attention deficits; but, unfortunately, those medications were not successful when administered to this group of children. Dr. Light emphasized that in most cases he had seen, the medicines made other symptoms worse. For example, children with autism who had some degree of involuntary and repetitive movements experienced an increase in these body movements when given ADHD medication. Dr. Light said for that reason, he did not recommend ADHD medication to his patients with autism.

His conclusion was that I should rely on the use of an effective behavior management plan and continue with her educational programming. This recommendation was a bitter pill to swallow. I felt as though the wheels had just fallen off all the hopes and anticipation I had set in motion. I had hoped to get some medication to supplement her education, interventions, and therapies. I came out of his office with more questions than answers.

If there were no medications for Teresa, how would I effectively address her behavior? What would I do about her slow progress in speech and language? Would she be able to live a semi-independent life if her current communication ability and her immature behavior were not effectively addressed now? I was determined to continue seeking whatever answers were available.

Teresa's Sensory Diet

Teresa, New York, in her pre-school classroom, wearing pink, lacy dress

Teresa, High School Graduation, May 2009,
Clear Lake High School, Houston, TX.

High School Graduation, May 2009, from
left to right-Ovie, Teresa, Elohor

Cincinnati, OH. 3rd grade, working with
the school's speech pathologist

Illustration of a Jaguar by Teresa, 2nd grade
science project, St. Louis, MO.

2004-Teresa's art collection on display in a hallway at
Amherst Regional High School, Amherst, MA, where she
completed her freshman year, before moving to Texas.

Art by Teresa. Abstract Portrait, inspired by 20th-Century French artist, Jean Metzinger

Teresa became a bona fide reader and developed a love for reading after she was held back in 2nd grade, St. Louis, MO.

Teresa's diagnosis inspired me to switch careers. In May 2000 I obtained my master's degree in special education from Xavier University, Cincinnati, OH.

Teresa on her high school graduation, May, 2009.

# Fourteen

## Cincinnati, Ohio
## 1997

In the summer of 1997, my family moved once again, this time to Ohio. Dele left his job in Missouri for further training in Cincinnati where he would begin a fellowship program in reproductive endocrinology and infertility.

It had now been almost eight years since we first arrived in America and I had been a stay-at-home mom throughout this period. However, because Teresa was now older, I decided it was time to transition back into the work force. I therefore enrolled at Xavier University, a private Jesuit university, to work toward a master's degree in education, specializing in special education and focusing on children with moderate to severe disabilities. Needless to say, Teresa was my inspiration for my chosen field. The training in special education would provide me with more know-how to help with her educational needs at home.

I find it interesting when I think of how quickly and easily I decided to change my career path for my child's sake. Back in Nigeria, with my MBA degree, I worked as a training officer in a steel corporation and had expected to continue in that career path when I immigrated to the

USA. But just like the saying goes, "Man proposes, but God disposes." I found myself switching careers without much thought. After I obtained my master's degree in special education in 2000, I started work as a special education teacher and have continued this work without any misgiving or regret. As a matter of fact, I could not have made a better choice. This is what I am supposed to be doing, and I feel blessed that I found my path in this unexpected way.

In Cincinnati we rented a three-bedroom townhouse in Anderson Township, a suburb of Cincinnati, and enrolled our children in the neighborhood public schools. Teresa and Ovie would begin third and sixth grades, respectively, while Elohor would begin eighth grade.

At her new elementary school, Teresa's academic programming was similar to that of Wren Hollow Elementary. She spent part of the day in an inclusive classroom and another part of the day in a resource room with a special education teacher. She was in the inclusive classroom for math and spelling, two subjects where she performed at grade level. In the resource room she worked on a new set of academic goals and objectives that included a focus on further progress in reading and writing.

Her math and reading skills continued to improve steadily, but it was her spelling ability that astounded me. She continued to excel in spelling—in a benchmark spelling assessment at the start of the year she spelled 43/50 words correctly, much to the surprise of her new inclusive teacher who had underestimated her. Most third-grade spelling words were difficult even for typical students to spell. For instance, the list included words with double consonants, which were usually tricky for many students to grasp and remember. Examples of third grade words that Teresa could easily spell included *really, lettuce, dribble,* and *happen.* Other words on the list included words with diagraphs, like /ch/ as in *choose* and /sh/ as in *shout.* Teresa spelled them all easily. She therefore, did not need any form of accommodation or modification for spelling. She was given the same expectation in spelling as her classmates and she scored 100%, or close, on all of her grade-level weekly spelling tests.

Regarding writing, though, she maintained her cursive handwriting skill and copied beautifully from the board; she had difficulty constructing her own sentences, something that was not a surprise, because of her expressive language deficit. Expressive language (speech) is linked to recording language (writing). There is a common phrase in educational circles that says, "If you can talk it, you can write it." Therefore, because Teresa's expressive language had not developed, she could not write.

Consequently, one of her IEP objectives was to be able to write a simple complete sentence with appropriate end punctuation and capitalization. To address this objective, the special education teacher first taught Teresa to recognize what a complete and correct sentence looked like and then to discriminate between a correct sentence and an incorrect sentence. One of the daily exercises she used to practice this skill was to correct short sentences for improper placement of capitals and end punctuation. For example, she could be given a sentence like this: *the cat is sad* and her job was to determine what was wrong with the sentence and fix it. In this case, she would be expected to capitalize the letter /t/ at the beginning of the sentence and insert a period after the word /sad/.

She was given about 10 minutes a day to practice sentence correction independently. She sometimes goofed off during her daily independent practice and needed a lot of verbal redirection to get back to work. In order to keep Teresa focused, the teacher created a positive behavior management system. She introduced the use of an oven timer to set a time limit for work completion. Teresa earned a sticker whenever she finished her work before the timer went off. This positive reinforcement worked well, not only because Teresa got a kick out of setting the timer herself, but also because she liked to collect stickers.

After the introduction of the timer, the teacher reported that Teresa would finish her class work before the timer went off as many as 3 out of 4 times weekly. Eventually, the timer was eased out when Teresa adapted to finishing her work in a timely manner. She still got her stickers though.

When my daughter became familiar with what a complete simple sentence looked like, she was ready to learn to write short sentences of her own. To achieve this, the teacher encouraged her to do a lot of free writing. Frequently, she was asked to draw a picture on paper and write a word, a phrase, or a short sentence about the picture.

Very quickly, Teresa became inspired to draw and write about anything she wanted in her journal. Initially, she drew beautiful pictures, including rainbows, hearts, and the sun (her favorite things to draw), but the words she wrote for the pictures bore no connection to them. Nevertheless, Teresa was praised for her efforts and encouraged to keep writing regardless.

She developed a love for writing during this time, and by fourth grade she started to write words and phrases that connected to her pictures. With more practice and time she improved to the point of writing short sentences and, eventually, short stories that only she could completely understand.

Inspirations for her story titles came from her home and school environments. Others came from picture storybooks she tried to read, but was unable to, in which case, she made up the stories herself by giving the pictures her own interpretations. I got the feeling that her stories would make for interesting reading, if only they could be understood.

One thing that made her writing hard to understand was a plethora of grammatical flaws. Many of her sentences consisted of a cacophony of nouns, verbs, and prepositions that did not always fit together properly. What I often wondered was whether her jumbled written words were a reflection of how her brain held or processed information, which would explain her confusion with conventional language. Her teachers and I concurred that as long as she kept writing, there was progress.

What she tried to convey in her writings could have been anybody's guess. In one of her more coherent writings, about her visit to the zoo, which she titled *The Animal Zoo*, she wrote about six animals, all of which she illustrated beautifully. This piece and my interpretation of it are outlined in a table below.

# The Animal Zoo

| Teresa's Story | My Interpretation |
|---|---|
| *Cat was Animal.* | The cat is an animal. |
| *Roef was Zoo.* | The dog was in the zoo (*Roef* being a dog's bark, representing the dog). |
| *Giraffe was Animals Zoo.* | The giraffe was in the animal zoo. |
| *Bunny was Animal.* | The bunny is an animal. |
| *Duck was quack quack quack.* | The duck quacked, quacked, and quacked. |
| *Turtle was zoo waters.* | The turtle was in the water at the zoo. |
| *The six animals zoos.* | These were six animals in the zoo. |
| *Goodbye animals.* | Goodbye, animals. |

Even though I could not understand her writings, her interest in writing, her ability to write words on paper, and her understanding of simple sentences were all encouraging. Her attempts to write stories, comprehensible or not, represented a significant milestone in her educational progress, because she could not do this back in St. Louis. Obviously, she was demonstrating a continued capacity to learn.

# Fifteen

## Cincinnati, Ohio
## 1997

**M**y eagerness for Teresa to continue to grow in her writing soared after seeing her progress. I reasoned that writing could become an alternate medium for communication, barring adequate speech development. Even so, I did not give up on her speech acquisition.

Her speech pathologist at her school was Mrs. Liz Abrahams, a woman I greatly admired. A part time PhD candidate, Mrs. Abrahams was a brilliant, energetic, and lively woman who exuded personal charm perfectly blended with professionalism. She had a great sense of humor and always had a smile on her face. To improve Teresa's ability to communicate through speech, Mrs. Abrahams explored a practical, hands-on approach to her therapy and continuously looked for new strategies that worked.

Some of Teresa's IEP objectives for speech that Mrs. Abrahams worked tirelessly to address included the following:

- *verbally requesting and commenting in complete sentences*
- *verbally responding to simple questions*
- *taking turns*

In therapy, learning tasks were broken down into small chunks, and skills were taught through engaging games. She facilitated numerous games between Teresa and her fellow speech-impaired mates in order to make therapy sessions fun and relevant. Mrs. Abrahams employed positive reinforcements, mostly in the form of giving praise or stickers to the students.

Working in collaboration with the special education teacher and me, Mrs. Abrahams made concrete plans for home reinforcement: she kept me informed of the particular skills Teresa was working on, as well as how they were being addressed, and then advised me on specific practices I could do at home with Teresa to reinforce each skill. For example, when they were working on the objective to *verbally respond to simple questions,* Mrs. Abrahams would send me a question that she wanted me to ask Teresa, as well as her expected response. She would rehearse the dialogue with Teresa during the therapy session that day, and that night at home Teresa was expected to respond to my question in a complete sentence while maintaining eye contact. One question was:

*"What game did you play with Mrs. Abrahams today?"*
Her expected response was to be:
*"I played a game with cards."*

This approach to therapy made for a successful school-to-home transfer of learning. In addition to suggesting specific ways to reinforce speech skills at home, Mrs. Abrahams kept me regularly updated on Teresa's progress, frequently sending me notes to apprise me of little successes and progress.

Once, she reported that she had asked if Teresa wanted to play ball with her, and Teresa had replied with an emphatic "No!" This simple response was worthy of applause. Under normal circumstances, Teresa usually walked away without a verbal response whenever anyone asked a question about something she had no interest in. On this particular day, Teresa not only verbally responded in the negative, she made a request of her own. She asked the therapist if she could play her favorite game, Mr. Potato Head and Pals. The therapist was so thrilled by her request that she granted her wish immediately.

Mrs. Abrahams also revealed that anytime Teresa's therapy group played Mr. Potato Head and Pals, Teresa was the model student. She took turns, requested game pieces appropriately, and conducted herself well, even when she did not win.

Mrs. Abrahams also used short, positive narratives known as Social Stories to teach social skills and appropriate behavior to Teresa. Developed by Carole Gray in 1991, the Social Stories were written primarily to teach children with autism how to respond appropriately to a given situation. The stories describe specific situations, such as how to use the bathroom, brush teeth, or play at recess.

Mrs. Abrahams explained Social Stories to me in detail. There are specific guidelines to follow when writing a Social Story. One of the guidelines is for the writer to consider the situation from the perspective of the child. The stories often include information that helps children with autism understand the feelings and thoughts of others. Teachers, therapists, parents, or any service providers can write a Social Story for classroom or home use. Teresa had several stories written for her by Mrs. Abrahams. One of them was titled "Playing at Recess." I think it helped my daughter finally understand the ins and outs of recess behavior.

Although I did not personally write a Social Story for Teresa at this time, after I became a special education teacher, and learned more about Social Stories, I wrote many Social Stories for my students and found them very effective. I actually had an occasion to write a social story for a mother of my student who requested it for home use. She wanted to mentally prepare her pre-teen daughter living with autism, for what to expect when her monthly period would start. The mother was quite nervous about this inevitable developmental milestone for young women. She was very pleased with the Social Story that I wrote to address the issue and it went a long way to reduce her anxiety.

In order to foster social skills, the speech pathologist also made plans for Teresa's involvement in group activities within her inclusive classroom. For instance, she ensured that Teresa participated in the morning class meetings with adequate support. During morning meetings, all the students sat in a circle and took turns singing a greeting song. The song went like this:

*My name is* _____ *Check!*
*They call me* _____ *Check!*
*I like to* _____ *Check!*
*That's what I like. Check!*

"*Check*" was the chorus chanted by the rest of the class, while each student took turn singing the lyrics and filling in the blanks. The special education teacher and Mrs. Abrahams alternately supported Teresa during this activity.

In the first couple of weeks of Teresa's participation in this activity, Mrs. Abrahams or the special education teacher sang for her whenever it was her turn because she was initially aloof. In time, she warmed up, and with prompts, she started to sing the lyrics and fill in the blanks by herself. Eventually, the responsibility for prompting her was shifted to her classmates, who by now were familiar with her and were eager to help.

The first time that she sang her song without prompts was a triumphant day! The special education teacher was so excited that she wrote a note home to tell me all about it. When Teresa came home that day, I celebrated by praising her and hugging her numerous times. I asked her to sing the song for me, but she was not as thrilled as I was and simply walked away.

The use of the telephone was another important life skill that the speech pathologist tried to teach Teresa through collaboration with the special education teacher and me. First, she taught Teresa to memorize our phone number by writing the number on a note card and having her say it over and over again daily. Teresa learned her phone number in no time. Next, using a play phone, the speech pathologist demonstrated how to dial numbers on a phone. After that, to practice how to make a real call, the pathologist made an arrangement for me to take a call from Teresa in school.

The pre-scheduled call home came on a Tuesday afternoon around 1:30. I picked up the phone and greeted Teresa by calling her name and identifying myself. She sounded excited the first time she heard my voice on the other end of the line. I did most of the talking and tried to prompt her to say something back to me. Then she voiced a few words and phrases that bore no bearing or relevance to the moment. I talked to her some more, after which we ended the call. This was a significant moment for me. I was thinking…. *My daughter, calling me on the phone!* Despite the fact that her words and phrases were few and made no sense, my heart danced a few bits. We had one more staged phone call after this initial one with a similar outcome.

In an effort to help Teresa maintain her newly acquired telephone skill, Mrs. Abrahams got a walkie-talkie to simulate the use of a telephone and used it to communicate with Teresa within the school environment. The device also encouraged my child to speak. She was so taken by this new device that she requested that we get one for her at home. So we bought her a toy set.

After teaching Teresa how to use the phone, Mrs. Abrahams also taught her to successfully memorize our home address.

Through all of this concentrated effort forward: the tantalizing technological tools of phones and walkie-talkies, and with a lot of repetition, the speech pathologist, the special education teacher, and I were able to inspire Teresa to gain more essential life skills: answering direct questions when prompted, knowing her phone number and home address, and having an understanding of what a phone was for. My child had taken another stride of integration into the communicative social world!

# Sixteen

## MORE SPEECH THERAPY

## Cincinnati, Ohio
## 1998

The benefits of the speech therapy sessions with Mrs. Abrahams were clear. I therefore felt that more significant gains in speech and language might be achieved through extended therapy. However, because of issues relating to caseloads and scheduling, the school could not provide the additional therapy time that I requested. So, I decided to find a private speech therapist outside of school.

The first place I contacted was the Cincinnati Children's Hospital Medical Center. To my pleasant surprise, I was told that they offered the service and that there was an outpatient location in our area, only fifteen minutes from where we lived. They said that I could take Teresa there for an initial evaluation and subsequent therapy. The news got even better when I was informed that our medical insurance would cover the cost of services. I was overjoyed.

In January 1998, I took Teresa to the speech pathology department at the Children's Outpatient East Facility in Cincinnati for her initial evaluation. The speech pathologist who examined her was a tall, kind-looking gentleman, Mr. Ivan Coleman. To assess Teresa's current language acquisition status, Mr. Coleman used a combination of personal observation and formal and informal assessment tools.

For the Receptive Language Assessment (ability to comprehend spoken language), Mr. Coleman's report stated that Teresa followed basic commands well, wrote primer or beginning words from dictation, and "drew an accurate representation of a girl and a house from a verbal command." Her weakness was in the understanding of questions beginning with *Who, Where, When,* and *What.* Although Mr. Coleman did not indicate the level of functioning of Teresa in the Receptive Language Assessment, my guess was that it was about the same or slightly higher than her Expressive Language ability.

For the Expressive Language Assessment (ability to express want and needs), the results indicated Teresa's level of functioning was around 4 years, 2 months old. Mr. Coleman noted that she requested objects using short phrases and did not initiate communication. However, she used greetings appropriately, and gave some personal demographic information accurately.

He concluded that at 9 years, 9 months, Teresa "demonstrated continued language and pragmatic deficits." He recommended "further enhancement of these skills as well as additional individualized training in order to achieve maximum gains and transfer of skills."

Two weeks after the evaluation, I met with one of the speech pathologists at the Cincinnati Children's Hospital outpatient center, Mrs. Jennifer London, a soft-spoken, patient woman whom Teresa liked very much. Mrs. London and I looked over the evaluation results and discussed possible goals and objectives to incorporate into a treatment plan.

We decided that treatment would start on February 20, about 3 weeks after our meeting. Mrs. London would see my child once a week for a 45-minute evening session. Teresa's main speech goal was to develop functional language. The objectives toward achieving the goal were as follows:

- *To increase expressive language that would include complete sentences in structured and spontaneous speaking situations;*
- *To accurately provide personal data information, both verbally and in writing;*
- *To increase understanding of causation "because" and time concepts (past and future);*
- *To demonstrate the ability to develop a story by using pictures and utilizing initiation, maintenance, and end;*
- *To provide appropriate responses for a variety of /WH/question forms.*

I thought that it would be beneficial if the school therapist and the hospital therapist worked together to implement these objectives. When I asked Mrs. London and Mrs. Abrahams separately what they thought about it, each jumped at the idea, so I introduced them. They took it from there and called each other to collaborate and work on the same goals for reinforcement purposes.

For the next twelve months, I drove Teresa to the clinic once a week in the evenings for her speech therapy session with Mrs. London. Each time, I sat in the waiting room and watched them through a glass window. Mrs. London used a variety of high interest games and books during therapy, and Teresa seemed to enjoy being with her.

Six months into the therapy, Mrs. London prepared a report on Teresa's progress toward the main goal and supporting objectives. The report indicated that Teresa had made steady progress toward her objectives, most notably in the area of expressive language. Teresa consistently used complete sentences during structured activities. Prompts that were needed initially had been phased out gradually. There was some carry-over to spontaneous speech, but it was not significant.

She was able to give more personal data information, both verbally and in written form, with a great degree of accuracy regarding her address, telephone number, her school's name, her age, and her birthday. She was also able to sequence pictures to a story and use complete sentences to tell the story in a structured setting.

All these successes notwithstanding, Teresa continued to struggle with answering *WH* question forms. One of the common errors that she made was a mismatch, when she answered a particular question as if a different question was asked. For example, she would answer a *when* question as if it were a *where* question.

Mrs. London tried hard to use visual supports to help my daughter understand *WH* questions. For instance, when Mrs. London asked Teresa a question from a picture story like, *"What is the cat doing?"* Mrs. London simultaneously pointed to a corresponding picture or symbol in the story to cue the correct response. In spite of the therapist's efforts, progress in this area was insignificant.

In addition to difficulty with *WH* question forms, Teresa continued to struggle with relating remote or past experiences. For example, my child was still unable to respond to a question like, *"What did you eat for lunch?"*

But overall, I was happy. Teresa was demonstrating progress in her speech acquisition due to the committed, collaborative effort of Mrs. Abrahams, Mrs. London, and me, as well as Teresa's cooperation and persistence of course. Mrs. London was able to address areas that Mrs. Abrahams was unable to tackle in school. It was also a chance for Teresa to transfer some of the skills she learned in school to other situations.

Getting additional speech therapy sessions from the children's hospital was one of the best decisions that I made regarding Teresa's education. As a result of our combined efforts, Teresa started to gradually use more spontaneous speech in everyday communication, though with one-word or two-word phrases at a time. Her gains in expressive communication enhanced Teresa's interactions with us at home. She could now say, "outside," when she wanted to go outside to play, as opposed to just running out the door without saying anything and having us react with alarm, wondering about her intention.

Teresa was visibly motivated and thrilled by her increasing ability to use language spontaneously. Now, more confident of her ability to speak a little bit, she giggled whenever she formulated a sentence to express a need and then looked at us to check for our reaction. When she spotted our awe-struck faces, her giggles graduated into boisterous laughter. Her elation over the ability to express herself in words was infectious, as we all joined her in uncontrollable laughter.

Her acquisition of some spontaneous speech was wonderful for me as well, as I had to guess less of the time as to what she wanted. Although it was a small step, it made a difference for Teresa and me. Unfortunately, as for the behavior issue, I would not say there was yet any significant improvement. One step at a time...

# Seventeen

BEHAVIOR DIFFICULTIES- A ROADBLOCK

## Cincinnati, Ohio
## 1999

Although Teresa was gaining academically and her teachers were marveling over her progress in reading, writing, math and spelling, they were not as thrilled about her behavior. They sent home reports that described her as restless, anxious, hyperactive, and inattentive. The reports noted that she did not follow directions well and did not always complete her assignments. Back in St. Louis, she had demonstrated some of these behaviors but not to the extent that was now being described to me.

A particularly troubling problem was that she would frequently cry spontaneously without apparent cause. On one occasion, I was even called to come and pick her up because they couldn't get her to stop crying. By the time I reached the school however, she had finally stopped, so it was not necessary to take her home.

I noticed also that for the first time Teresa no longer enjoyed going to school. She started feigning illness just to avoid going. I was not sure why and didn't know what to do.

The principal and staff didn't seem to know what to do either. I do not think they had much experience working with the challenging behaviors that can manifest from children with autism. So, they did what they knew at the time. The principal called me to a meeting and handed me a detailed, two-page behavior contract, which her team had drafted to address Teresa's misbehavior. The document listed all of Teresa's misbehaviors, the consequences attached to them, and the potential rewards for desired behaviors. They asked me to read the document and sign it.

As I was perusing the paper, the principal, who was visibly annoyed over Teresa's conduct, asked if Teresa was aggressive or if she had ever hurt anyone. Astounded, I told her that of course my child was not aggressive and had never hurt anyone. The principal then warned me that if Teresa ever cried again, I would be called and Teresa would be sent home promptly. She further cautioned that Teresa would not be allowed to return to the school if she continued her crying spells and continued to act inappropriately.

To say that I was stunned would be underestimating the range of emotions I was going through. Apparently this school administrator viewed the crying as misconduct, whereas I saw it as a child with ASD in distress needing empathy and attention. The principal's threat to prevent a child with autism from attending school because she cried was confusing to me, to say the least. Too dumbfounded to construct a proper response, and unsure what else to do, I silently signed the document presented to me, apologized for my child's misbehavior (though with internal misgivings as their stance felt unfair), and promised to do whatever I could to improve the situation. I left the meeting feeling very downhearted.

Suffice it to say, the behavior contract did nothing to improve Teresa's behavior simply because it was poorly conceived. In my current capacity as a trained special education teacher, I now know that behavior contracts are one of the most effective tools to positively shape children's behavior, but only if the contracts are appropriately designed. A behavior contract is most effective when tailored specifically for each child in an easily understandable fashion that allows the child to take ownership.

A contract's language and goals must be formed at the child's level of development so that he or she can relate to its purpose and thus be willing to try to regulate behavior in order to earn appropriate and specific rewards.

Teresa's contract at her school was not created for her understanding and buy-in, but rather for the educators who implemented it. She did not even know that she had a behavior contract.

I instinctively knew that what my child needed was an empathetic, therapeutic, and rehabilitative approach to her issues, but the school administration— understandably due to lack of knowledge of ASD at that time— was unable to provide appropriate services for her.

Teresa's behavior challenges and the response by the school continued to upset me a great deal.

I know first-hand how hard it is for teachers to work with a student who exhibits restlessness, anxiety, hyperactivity, and inattentiveness in the classroom. I get that. But I felt it was important for anyone working with Teresa to understand that her behavior could not be separated from her brain dysfunction, and, invariably, from her functional age. The experience with this administration led me to feel that children with autism can be too quickly cast aside since their brain dysfunction is not visible to the eye like a broken leg or other physical challenge. Unfortunately, the most evident aspects of ASD are the symptoms that least fit in with social norms.

At around this time, I heard about Applied Behavior Analysis, (ABA), a behavior intervention used for children with Autism Spectrum Disorders and related disabilities, to teach appropriate behaviors, including speech, academics and life skills. In my current capacity as an educator of children with special needs, I have personal knowledge of the fact that ABA is now considered best practice among ASD behavior experts.

In 2000, when my family moved to Amherst, Massachusetts, I tried to get the ABA intervention for my child through private means; but, when I contacted a private treatment center in Northampton, Massachusetts,

I was told that their ABA intervention was geared for children younger than ten. Teresa was twelve.

The lack of appropriate interventions to address my daughter's behavior at the Cincinnati school fueled my zeal to continue to find effective treatment for her symptoms. I knew it was a long shot, but I resolved to keep trying. Her behavior had to be brought under control in order to optimize her ability to learn.

# Eighteen

## Sensory Integration Disorder (SID)

## Amherst, Massachusetts
## 2000-2001

In 2000 my family relocated to New England where we settled down in Amherst, Massachusetts. Ever on the move due to work opportunities, my husband, Dele, and I had completed our training in Cincinnati in our respective fields and subsequently obtained jobs in Springfield, MA. We chose to live in the quaint university town of Amherst, which is about fifty minutes from Springfield. Teresa, then twelve years old, joined the sixth grade at Wildwood Elementary School.

Not long after we had hung our curtains in the windows of our new home and arranged our pictures on the walls, Teresa received a new diagnosis at school that offered a different lens through which to view and understand our daughter's symptoms.

The role in which Sensory Integration Dysfunction (SID) plays in influencing the behavior of ASD children was either unknown or not fully understood by the administration at her school during the time we were in Cincinnati, (1997-2000). Consequently, behavioral expectations for children living with autism tended to be higher than what nature allows them to execute. Although Dr. Light in St. Louis had mentioned briefly in his assessment report that Teresa was "ultra-sensitive to tactile stimuli, especially around the face and head," I did not yet fully understand the impact of SID and did not consider it as a possible root cause when confronted with Teresa's behavioral challenges.

However, around November of 2000, the occupational therapist in Teresa's new school administered an assessment that revealed that Teresa's longtime behavioral issues were due in large part to SID, a condition that commonly occurs alongside ASD. The autism consultant at the school requested the assessment after a discussion I had with her, during which I shared some of Teresa's odd behaviors at home, like: crying without apparent cause, inattentiveness, hyperactivity, and irritation with the sound of running water.

The autism consultant explained SID to me this way: sensory integration dysfunction causes unique problems with processing sensory information—sight, sound, smell, taste, touch—as well as causes difficulties with positional sensation or sense of movement.

She said that with SID the brain filters sensory input in such a way that certain senses may be highly attuned to stimuli, while other senses are less responsive than normal. For example, a person with SID may have an extreme reaction to a mild smell in a room that every other person can comfortably ignore. A whisper may sound like a yell, while a yell feels like one's eardrums are about to explode. Normal lighting in a room may be bothersome, or a fascinating light pattern coming through a window might arrest attention to the point of filtering out all else. A person with SID may have great difficulty blocking out simultaneous minor distractions in a room, such as the hum of a clock, people talking a few feet away, or a blinking light, so that everything vies for attention at the same time. Consequently, focusing becomes a problem.

When I learned about SID, it was like putting on a new pair of prescription glasses; suddenly all the edges that had appeared fuzzy were in sharp focus. Finally, Teresa's past and current behaviors made perfect sense—her hyperactivity, lack of focus, inattention, restlessness, agitations, anxiety, spontaneous screaming or crying, and the other un-usual reactions she had to what seemed like benign situations or environ-ments. I now had a formal name for and scientific research to support what I had intuitively sensed all along.

Author and professor Temple Grandin is a highly successful woman with ASD who holds a PhD in animal science. She explains in her no-table book *Animals in Translation* that animals and many people with autism possess the ability to discern minute visual details in their sur-roundings that typical kids and adults routinely miss. In this regard they possess hyper-specific intelligence and tend to be strong visual thinkers who process information primarily in pictures.

To illustrate, Grandin shares that cattle walking through a cattle chute will often spook, and the handler will have no idea why. All the handler sees is the plain old cattle chute; everything looks the same as every other day. The cattle, however, will spy the small plastic shopping bag flapping suspiciously on the fence rail that wasn't there the last time they walked through the chute.[viii]

Those living with ASD tend to have similar hyper-specific sense per-ception. In fact, Grandin's strong visual awareness earned her notoriety for her work advising livestock handlers and designing animal-friendly, humane farm facilities.

Grandin shares that she herself thinks solely in pictures. "During my thinking process I have no words in my head at all, just pictures."[ix] Grandin goes on to explain, "I always find it kind of funny that normal people are always saying autistic children 'live in their own little world.' When you work with animals for a while you start to realize you can say the same thing about normal people. There's a great big, beautiful world out there that a lot of folks are just barely taking in . . . Normal people literally don't see a lot of things."[x]

With SID, this sensual acuity may manifest in any or all of the five senses. Those with SID may feel significant physical discomfort when touched or hugged, as though sandpaper were being rubbed on their skin. For years I had felt my child's resistance to or lack of interest in my hugs. She did not like it when I combed her hair either. No matter how gently I tried to comb it, she could not tolerate the discomfort. She often cried or ran away whenever she saw a comb in my hand. I accommodated this problem by brushing with a soft hairbrush instead of combing.

Washing her face during showers was also a problem. As a remedy, I gently sponged her face with a washcloth rather than allow water to drip down her face from her head, which, her protests showed, was too much for her to handle. I shampooed her hair by tipping her head slightly backward, and then washed her hair using a backward motion in such a way that water could not run down her face. She also did not like any form of lotion on her skin, so I accommodated her by only lightly moisturizing her legs and hands.

Auditory sensitivity was particularly bothersome to Teresa too. Sometimes she reacted to irritating noises with significant distractibility and hyperactivity. At other times, she acted out, cried, screamed or ran away from auditory stimulation. The sound of running water in a sink or a flushing toilet bothered her so much that whenever she heard the sound, she ran away as fast as she could. It's easy to see why showers or baths were an issue! Whenever she was about to flush a toilet, she looked like someone preparing to light a match in a pool of kerosene. She would position herself for flight by standing astride. Then, standing a few feet from the flush lever, she would lean forward and stretch one hand toward the lever to push it down. The second she lifted her hand off the lever she blocked her ears with both hands and sprinted out of the bathroom.

Teresa's unusual sensitivity to sound also manifested as an acute sense of hearing. One summer evening our family was relaxing in the living room when Teresa suddenly repeated over and over again, "fire truck," "fire truck," "fire truck." We neither saw nor heard any fire trucks and did not know what to make of her words, so we ignored her. Several minutes later, we heard a fire truck pass by our house wailing its loud siren. It was only then that it became clear to us that she had heard it long before any of us had heard it.

Sometimes, even the sound of my voice became bothersome. When I spoke in my regular voice, or at least what seemed regular to me, she would cover her ears with her hands and say, "Whisper, Mommy, whisper." When I whispered, she was fine.

Teresa also had other sensory-related behaviors such as excessive movement and frequent rocking. The occupational therapist explained that there were times when some of Teresa's behaviors indicated either "sensory-seeking" or "sensation-avoiding" behaviors. For instance, if she began to spin or rock, it was a sensory-seeking behavior because she was under-stimulated and was trying to adjust to her sensitivity to the environment. In contrast, when she was hyperactive or acting out, it meant she was over-stimulated and needing a reduction of stimulation.

The therapist told me that during under-stimulation, when Teresa was rocking or spinning, I should allow her to do so or guide her to an alternative way to regulate her body, because the rocking and spinning were fulfilling a necessary function for her body's system. This was so important for me to know, because my inclination before had been to stop her from rocking because it had seemed an "atypical" movement.

The idea of seeking sensation due to under-stimulation might also be an explanation for her love of freedom and playing outdoors. In that environment, she can more easily regulate her own sensations.

I should mention here that in public places, the rocking and spinning of children with autism may draw unwanted attention to the children from people who do not understand what is going on. So, it might be necessary to teach the children alternative or replacement behaviors which can fulfil the same benefit as the rocking and spinning. The special education teacher, the autism consultant, or the school psychologist at the child's school might be able to assist parents with the training.

In order to better regulate Teresa's whole sensory system, and to foster sensory stimulation, our therapist recommended we engage Teresa in regular basic yoga movements and swimming.

In addition, Teresa was also placed on a "sensory diet" plan. Sensory Diet is described very well by authors Lindsey Biel, M.A., OTR/L and Nancy Pesk in their book, *Raising A Sensory Smart Child,* from which the following excerpts were shared:

> Just as your child needs food throughout the course of the day, the need for sensory input must also be met. A "sensory diet" (coined by OT Patricia Wilbarger) is a carefully designed, personalized activity plan that provides the sensory input a person needs to stay focused and organized throughout the day. Just as you may jiggle your knee or chew gum to stay awake or soak in a hot tub to unwind, children need to engage in stabilizing, focusing activities too. Infants, young children, teens, and adults with mild to severe sensory issues can all benefit from a personalized sensory diet.[xi]

Biel and Pesk go on to write:

> Each child has a unique set of sensory needs. Generally, a child whose nervous system is over-aroused and too wired, needs more calming input, while the child who is more under-aroused and too tired needs more alerting input. A qualified occupational therapist can use her or his advanced training and evaluation skills to develop a strong sensory diet for your child—or you—but it's up to you and your child to implement it throughout the day.

Teresa's sensory diet plan consisted of a variety of relaxing sensory activities that she undertook throughout the day at prescheduled intervals to ease stress or to help modulate her feelings and emotions. The activities were custom-made to be things that she typically liked to do, including listening to music, taking a walk, swinging, eating a snack, playing computer games, relaxing on a hammock, sitting on a rocking chair, sharpening pencils, doing push-ups, and erasing the board.

In school, the occupational therapist and Teresa's aide ensured that Teresa had access to some of these activities at pre-determined times throughout the school day.

The therapist also advised that Teresa be exposed to a variety of textures in order to increase her tolerance to touch and to reduce sensitivity. During therapy at school, the therapist frequently applied lotion to Teresa's skin. She also manicured her nails and gave her pedicures. The manicures and pedicures were, surprisingly, a hit for Teresa. Although she did not like to be touched, she tolerated having her nails and toes done because she liked the beautiful outcome, or perhaps because her love for art and beauty was strong enough to enable her to overcome her aversion for touch.

I was also informed about other ways I could help my child regulate stimulation when she appeared anxious or agitated over something at home. One of the strategies was to play light music in the background, keep the light low, and wrap her with a blanket. Then I hugged her tight and rocked back and forth, like in a hammock. I could tell that my daughter liked this position because I felt her body relax and her anxiety gradually faded.

At other times, as she lay beside me on the bed while I read a book to her, I would pile a couple of pillows on top of her and place some more at her sides, such that she was in a pillow cocoon. This also had a calming effect on her. There were times she would even request or initiate this form of therapy.

This sensory solution to regulate stimulation worked for my child, because it involved sustained, firm pressure (something which calms people with ASD), as opposed to other kinds of touch, such as light pressure, or direct touching of the skin, which may cause discomfort or irritation.

To survive her adolescence, Temple Grandin relates constructing her own "squeeze suit" to calm herself down. She borrowed the idea from a squeeze chute she saw veterinarians using to administer treatment to cattle. At first her machine only consisted of plywood boards and an air compressor! Eventually she added some cushioning. In her book she shares the following:

> All autistic children and adults like deep pressure. Some of them will put on really tight belts and hats to feel the pressure, and lots of autistic children like to lie underneath sofa cushions and even have a person sit on top of the cushions. I used to like to go under the sofa cushions when I was little. The pressure relaxed me.[xii]

Teresa's SID diagnosis was such a relief for Teresa's educators and for our family, because it brought with it new strategies for working with some of Teresa's behavioral issues and quite possibly addressed their root cause: heightened sensation and perception experienced to such a degree causing sensory overload and resulting in crying out or acting out for relief. Now we had some semblance of an understanding of what she was feeling and knew which proven actions we could take to assist her during those uncomfortable moments.

The day-to-day effect of this new knowledge on the family, particularly her siblings, was that Teresa's "poor" behavior was now met with sympathy rather than impatience or resentment.

# Nineteen

LITTLE BREAKTHROUGHS

## Amherst, Massachusetts
## 2000–2001

While Teresa behaved better within consistent structure and routine, surprisingly, she did not have any issues with our move to Amherst and all of our previous and subsequent relocations. We moved six or seven times after coming to America due to Dele's medical positions; and during the moves, Teresa did not throw fits or create upheavals of any sort.

Whenever we visited a new school in a new town, she wanted to explore the building. She wanted to know where the library, the lunchroom, her classroom, and the office were. So whenever I had to register her, I often asked the office staff to show us around first. For my child, it was always business as usual when any first day of school rolled around. I suspect that her sense of adventure sometimes trumps her need for routine. Whether or not that is true, this worked for all of us amidst the myriad of pressures of frequently relocating to a new place.

Teresa adjusted quickly and easily to Wildwood Elementary, and thus, her academic progress continued steadily. She could navigate her way around the building effortlessly by the second day and appeared to warm up to her new classmates. By the end of the first week of school Teresa had learned all of their names.

Her IEP team set goals for reading, writing, math, speech, social skills, and community skills. She spent part of her day in the special education resource classroom for reading and writing and the other part of her day in the inclusive classroom, where, in addition to math and spelling, she was exposed to a large variety of subjects, including science, social studies, cooking, music, computer technology, and physical education. The general education teacher, the special education teacher, and Teresa's personal aide worked together to modify and adapt her assignments as needed.

Very early on, my child emerged as a star in her spelling class. In that class, small groups of students often sat together creating word searches and puzzle games with their spelling words. Over time, Teresa got into it and became very good at this. She was usually the first one in her small group to finish using all of her words to create a word search and a puzzle, while other students were still struggling with theirs.

Because she was so good, the teacher picked Teresa to be the "lead puzzle creator" in her group. Her job as a lead puzzle creator was not only to assist her fellow students in completing their puzzles, but also to organize all of the puzzles and word searches created by her group. Sometimes I yearned to be a fly on the wall of that classroom, because I would have liked to see how she communicated with those students she was helping. I guess where there is a will, there is a way!

At about the same time, her teachers got Teresa involved in the Reading Buddy program to help her sustain interest in reading and to continue to develop confidence. Reading Buddy was an activity where students in higher grades were paired with students in lower grades for scheduled read-aloud sessions. The older students read to the younger students or vice versa. Whenever Teresa's inclusive classroom was scheduled to visit a lower classroom for Reading Buddy, Teresa went along. To support Teresa in this activity, the teachers assigned a non-disabled classmate to partner with her. They both visited a first grade classroom together, where they jointly read to a child. Her teacher told me that Teresa often came out of the reading sessions energized and motivated to read more.

As an added boost, to simultaneously enhance reading skills and develop language, the special education teacher integrated the students' speech goals into their reading activities. For instance, the teacher created a segment called "Talking," a time when students took turns to talk about a given topic. Talking time gave Teresa and other students with similar speech deficits the opportunity to practice speech skills. Question forms (*who, what, when, why, where*) were used to prompt the children to comment on a variety of topics. For example, one of the topics they commented on was, "What is the meaning of a best friend?"

It was during one of these talk activities that Teresa had a rare coherent conversation with her special education teacher that lasted more than mere seconds. Responding to a question about what she would do the coming weekend, she told the teacher about going to the "store" with "mummy" and going to "eat at Burger King." She also said she would be shopping at "Toys R Us." When the teacher told me about this, I confirmed that all of the information was true. We were thrilled that her information was relayed orally, using a combination of phrases and words. It was also accurate, meaningful, and within the right context.

It was remarkable that my child was twelve years old and here I was celebrating her ability to interact with her teacher for bare seconds, using a combination of single words and a phrase. This realization was as humbling as it was encouraging. From then on, I began to notice more instances when Teresa spoke spontaneously. For instance, she surprised me one day when in the dentist's chair, she yelled out to the dentist and staff working on her.

"Call my mom. I want my mom!" she said.

She could not see me from the dentist's chair, because I had stepped out to the hallway; so, she called out for me to come "save" her from having her fillings done. Though it was not the best of circumstances, I was happy to hear her spontaneously voice her plea in a complete sentence.

As part of her ongoing therapy, the speech therapist at Wildwood created fun opportunities to stimulate and improve the oral language of Teresa and her peers. The most popular activity was centered on cooking desserts. Through the course of the year, the students prepared different kinds of desserts, including chocolate puddings, cherry jellies, rice crispy squares, pumpkin pies, cupcakes with frosting and sprinkles, strawberry milkshakes, iced drinks with peaches, and a variety of cookies.

Anytime the group prepared desserts, the therapist talked to them throughout the process. Then she encouraged the students to pick their favorite dessert and explain what they liked about it and how to make it. At the end of the session, they typed their preferred recipe and took it home to their parents. The parents were encouraged to prepare the recipe at home with their child while again talking through the process. That way, they would reinforce the vocabulary and speaking skills learned in school.

This activity got Teresa's attention because it centered on food, which she loves. The teacher reported, "Teresa actively participates in the clean-up afterwards. She particularly likes to clean up the table and often volunteers to do so." It made me think.... *why doesn't she do the same at home?*

During the year, my daughter's program also provided opportunities to learn community and life skills. The special education teacher took her students in small groups to the grocery store weekly. The trip provided multiple avenues for the students to learn and reinforce life skills, such as crossing the street, paying for an item in the store with the correct amount of money, and communicating appropriately with members of the community.

Teresa loves to shop, especially for food! These weekly ventures to the store were the highlights of Teresa's school days. In preparation for the shopping trip, Teresa and her aide carefully made a shopping list for her inclusive class and speech therapy group. On the list they included snacks for the class as well as ingredients that Teresa's speech group would use for making desserts for that week. Teresa was also given the responsibility of going into the kindergarten classrooms to pick up any grocery lists that they might have. She then typed three separate lists: one for the kindergarten class, another for the inclusive class, and the last for the speech group. She also typed her own personal list, for which I gave her five dollars each week.

Inside the store, where her aide once fondly described my child as "gone a little wild," Teresa wanted to buy everything, but the aide always reminded her that they must stick with the list.

The weekly trips to the grocery store had a nice side benefit, because my daughter was introduced to the idea of creating a shopping list and sticking with it. To this day she and I always write a list before we go shopping; and, when she gets carried away and wants things outside of the list, I gently remind her that we have to stick with the list and she quietly accepts. When she gets home, she adds the items that she could not get onto the next list and waits patiently for our next shopping trip. This process has made our shopping trips very easy and I credit the community skills class for it.

I smile now when I think back to her tantrum outside the store near our apartment in New York when she was little. If only we'd had a list! By now I was seeing that the course towards achieving a fulfilling, successful life for my child involved many little victories born of an increasingly deeper understanding of the ways that she experienced her environment and other people, rather than one giant breakthrough that would solve all of her ASD symptoms and challenges.

# Twenty

MISGUIDED CHILDREN (AND PARENTS)

## Amherst, Massachusetts
## 2000-2001

Although my daughter's education in school was going well, unfortunately, we could not say the same about her experiences outside of school in Amherst. And though I am reluctant to write about this, it is an important issue that needs to be talked about, as part of her whole educational experience. The ostracization and bullying of children with special needs are of great concern to me, more so, because my child was a victim of both. For this reason, I have devoted the next two chapters to describe our experiences with these unfortunate issues.

After school, Teresa enjoyed playing outdoors at the Mill Valley apartment complex, where we had rented a three-bedroom apartment. She rode her bike most of the time. Other times we took walks together. There was a housing complex adjacent to ours, and both complexes shared common grounds where all the children played together. Teresa did not play with the other kids much, but she liked to hang out near some students she recognized from her school and watch them play.

She could not interact with these children because of her speech limitations; so, when they tried to interact with her, she said nothing, although she acknowledged them by smiling. She liked their attention.

Sadly, when some children noticed that Teresa was different, they rejected her outright. This disheartening fact came to my attention one evening when I heard a knock on my door. When I answered and stepped outside, a woman who I recognized to be a parent of one of the children living in the adjacent apartment complex was standing there with a serious expression on her face.

"I need to let you know something," she said, like she was resolved to reveal a large secret after much thought.

Instinctively, I knew whatever she had to say was not going to be good because she was not smiling.

"It's about your daughter," she continued. "I am telling you for your own good. The parents and children at my housing complex do not want your child around them. She needs to stay away from there."

"Excuse me, what?" I said. I thought for a moment that I misunderstood what she said.

Observing my confused facial expression, she elaborated. First, she repeated her warning that it was in my best interest to prevent my child from visiting her apartment complex because the people there did not like my child. Then she confided in me that one parent had threatened that she would call the police the next time they saw Teresa hanging around their area.

She further cautioned that the hatred for Teresa was so strong that she feared the children might even hurt her. Apparently, a small group of children frequently picked on Teresa; they laughed at her and drove her away whenever she came too close to them.

I was bewildered and disconcerted to say the least. I did not expect such mean treatment from young children, many of whom were Teresa's age, let alone such an attitude from the parents. I woodenly thanked the woman for her information, not even sure what to say to correct the misperception of my daughter. After she left, I could not help but wonder what in the world the parents were afraid of.

The next day, with my child's safety first and foremost on my mind, I walked over to the apartment complex. The morning was bright and sunny—a complete antithesis to the ugliness of the attitude I was on my way to confront. I was bewildered by the fear the woman had relayed, yet resolved to assure the parents I had heard their warnings. For her own wellbeing, Teresa would not be setting foot on their complex any more. More importantly, I hoped to educate them about Teresa and autism, because their ignorance was evoking unnecessary and unfounded fear, which is often at the root of prejudiced behavior.

Upon arrival at the complex, I did not see the woman who had come to my door. I was informed that she was at work, as were most of the other parents. However, I saw a younger woman on her porch where she was attending to a small boy. A slightly older girl with short brown hair and wearing a sundress was playing nearby with a pail of water on the sandy ground.

When I told the young mother why I had come, she expressed surprise and sympathy and said that she was not aware of the sentiments expressed by the other parents. She had seen Teresa around a few times and had noticed that she did not speak, but was never threatened by her presence.

Following our brief discussion, I asked her to inform the other parents that they need not worry, because my child would not be stepping foot on their complex again. I asked her to relay that Teresa was simply a child with autism and speech impairment; thus, their fear was unfounded.

"Just because she was born with a disability, doesn't make her a bad person," I said. "She is just like any other kid. She just wants to belong."

"I understand," she said, grabbing her toddler's hand right before he touched a bee that had landed on her geranium. "I'll be happy to explain."

"Thank you," I said, my tension rushing out of me.

When I looked back as I headed towards our complex grounds, the woman was watching me, still holding her boy's hand, her face pinched with concern.

As I crossed the green lawn, I was downcast. In the days following, whenever I saw kids playing outside, I felt bad that Teresa's freedom to associate with fellow neighborhood children was restricted by my fear for her safety. I was so concerned that I would not even allow her take a walk or ride her bike unless I was by her side watching out for her. It saddened me even more when she asked me why I wouldn't allow her to go outside to play. I did not know what to say to her. What good would it do to tell her the truth? I didn't wish to plant the seeds of fear and resentment in her young heart. I wanted to preserve her joy and innocence a bit longer.

Misjudgments such as the ones displayed by the parents of those children trouble me more than the behaviors of the kids themselves. I believe that the behaviors of children are a function of the environment in which they are raised. My concern is that if the parents are ignorant, then who will educate the children and teach them respect and tolerance for people that are different? I fear that such children will grow up to be just like their parents.

# Twenty-One

## TERESA TURNS THE TABLES

### Cincinnati, Ohio
### 1997-2000

We had a similar experience with misguided children back in Cincinnati, but Teresa did something that made me proud. She turned the tables; sort of.

Many children lived in our Anderson Township subdivision and they played outside together every evening and on the weekends. Because Teresa was unable to engage in conversation, the neighborhood kids mostly ignored her. Even so, while many of the children were kind and protective of Teresa, a small group among them was mean to her. When they figured out that she was different, they decided to entertain themselves by making her the butt of their jokes and an object of ridicule.

One day, my son Ovie, who was very protective of Teresa, witnessed a disturbing example of this bullying. The school bus had dropped off the children at the subdivision gate, and all of them, including Teresa and my son, were walking down in small groups along a narrow path to the residences.

As they walked, one boy in Teresa's group told her to pick up a dead rat that was lying on the ground. Another boy in the group did not like what he heard and quickly ran back to tell Ovie, who was with another group of students walking behind Teresa's group. Ovie's lightening intervention prevented Teresa from picking up the rat. If not for him, it was highly likely that she would have done as the boy asked and who knows what the boy would have asked her to do with it? This might seem like a fairly minor incident, but picking up a dead rodent would have been a potential danger to my daughter's health. Teresa was naïve and gullible. She wanted to be their friend, so she would do anything they asked, even if their requests were unkind.

At other times, my son would hear some of these particular kids call Teresa names like "retarded" and "stupid."

I personally saw a boy use a water hose to spray water on Teresa one day as the children were playing outside. This boy didn't know that I was watching from a distance. I was horrified as he directed the hose right at Teresa and sprayed her face at close range. I rushed over and asked him to stop. Surprised, he turned red with embarrassment and guilt, apologizing profusely. I accepted his apology and asked him not to do it again.

Worried about these negative incidents, I began to limit Teresa's outside playtime. However, Teresa eventually did something that earned her the respect of the children at our subdivision and won back her freedom to play outside more frequently.

Weekend bicycle races had become quite the popular activity in the neighborhood, both for spectators of all ages and the young participants. Just about all of the kids zealously joined in. The race winner got to enjoy a moment in the limelight and was greeted with cheers and rousing applause from parents and friends.

Initially, Teresa did not participate in the bike races for a couple of reasons. First, I was protective of her. I feared that she might get shoved or hurt in the rush and frenzy. Second, she did not have a bike. Her old bike with training wheels was broken, and I was procrastinating buying her a new bike. I was waiting for when I would have the time to teach her to ride without training wheels, which I anticipated would require some intense instruction and practice.

For a long time, Teresa stood on the sidelines and watched her brother and the other children race their bikes. All the while, and unbeknownst to me, she was nursing a fervent desire to ride a bike like the rest of the children. So, just like she had done many years prior when she weaned herself off diapers, my daughter did not wait for me to get around to providing the chance; she took matters into her own hands.

One evening, Teresa simply picked up an unattended bicycle, climbed onto it, and pedaled away smoothly and steadily like a pro. My neighbor, who observed this in awe, ran over to my house and told me. The two of us broke down laughing at my daughter's gumption. The very next day I bought her a new bicycle. Delighted, Teresa would ride her new bike all day on weekends and on weekday evenings until she could barely see beyond her nose and the dark of night forced her to quit.

After she got her new bike, Teresa participated in many neighborhood bike races, enjoying finally being a part of the group. One Saturday she showed up for another race and nonchalantly positioned herself, as usual, at the end corner of the crowd of racers, behind many eager kids who pushed her out of their way to get a good starting place. No one expected that anything unusual was about to happen.

The race began and she took off from the starting line, pedaling as hard as she could. We watched her pass a group of riders and push on, legs pumping furiously, a look of determination on her face. She passed a few more kids, steering her bike left and right to avoid several racers in front of her. People started cheering as she continued to overtake more riders. To our astonishment, she gradually moved up the line of kids, closing in on the frontrunners. As the racers bore down towards the finish line, the jaws of everyone watching dropped when Teresa surged forward and beat all the riders to win the race. It seemed so surreal. The underdog had won!

All the neighbors, even her tormenters, clapped and cheered and hooted and whistled for her. She responded to the acclaim with a very wide smile. From that day on the children at our subdivision, particularly the ones who were mean to her, did not look at her the same way again. She had earned their respect in her typical persevering, surprising fashion. All I could think was: *WOW! What a determined young lady my daughter is becoming.*

# Twenty-Two

## Amherst, Massachusetts
## 2001

In the middle of her sixth-grade year, we received an academic report from Teresa's teachers at Wildwood that noted, "Good progress." They acknowledged her sense of humor, and said that she was easy to work with. Other attributes credited to my child included an ability to work well in small groups, organizational skills, a good memory, strong skills in technology, and an aptitude for following routines independently. After reading the contents of the progress report at my kitchen table, I took a sip of my tea and exhaled a long breath. My daughter was doing so much better. I was quite pleased. The snow piled outside of my window suddenly seemed much brighter on that cold winter's morning.

The winter semester of the 2000-2001 school year went by quickly and in June 2001, Teresa achieved a milestone—her sixth grade graduation. To mark the occasion for the graduating class, the school community organized an elaborate ceremony. During the days leading up to the graduation, students and staff alike were buzzing like bees around their hives as they prepared for the special event.

The festive school atmosphere had Teresa excited as well. Whenever she got home from school, she would say to me, "Graduation?"

"Yes, Teresa is going to graduation," I would reply, smiling. She would laugh out loud and ask the same question over and over again.

On the day of her graduation, she wore a pretty lilac floral two-piece dress and a pair of black shoes, which we had bought especially for the event.

*Oh my God!* I thought as I looked at my daughter. *She looks just like a young lady!*

She looked different, because she hardly ever dressed up, preferring to wear shorts, tees, and tennis shoes at all times. She also appeared to be pleased with her new lady-like attire.

When we arrived at the school, Teresa walked proudly to the front of the event hall, where she was met by her school aide who walked her to an assigned seat among the rest of the graduates. I sat with the rest of the parents on one side of the hall.

The agenda included several entertaining performances by non-graduating students and sentimental speeches by staff members. First, the principal welcomed everyone and expressed her pride in the graduating class. Emotional staff speeches followed with each educator reminiscing about what a wonderful year they'd had with the graduating students, with an overall sentiment of how much they would miss these children who were now moving on to the next phase of growing up.

During intermission, soft music played in the background while photographs of each graduating student, spanning infancy to sixth grade, were projected on a large screen. It was a beautiful, moving sight.

As the photos slowly rolled across the giant screen, there were no dry eyes in the hall. The cute infant and toddler pictures of these now grown sixth graders demonstrated how far they had come, from days in diapers to now hopeful, confident, and mostly precocious pre-teens.

The photos were arranged in alphabetical order and because Teresa's last name ended with a Z, her photos were the last to roll out. Teresa's face lit up with excitement when she saw herself on the screen. The last picture, taken at her pre-school in New York City during a Christmas celebration, was especially gorgeous. In the photo, she wore a frilly pink lace dress that had a gathered waist, and to me, she looked as radiant as a princess. The teachers who put the slideshow together must have liked this photo too, because they reserved it for last and left it on the screen for the duration of the event.

When the time finally came, the graduating students filed in a line from the back of the hall to the front to receive their diplomas from their principal. Parents snapped multiple photographs of their beaming children.

Teresa was giggling with excitement as she walked alongside her aide. When she drew closer to the stage to meet the principal, she could no longer control her excitement, so her laughs grew louder and louder. At that point, her elation was simply too hard to contain, so she resorted to flapping her hands, rocking her head, and laughing out loud. The following words from the occupational therapist floated through my mind: *When she is hyperactive or acting out, it means she is over-stimulated and needs a reduction of stimulation.*

Her uncontrolled laughter and excitement caused her to lose her balance, so she repeatedly fell out of her position in line. Oddly, her behavior was a contrast to her lady-like outfit. Each time she stepped out of line, I could see the aide guide her back on track and try to hush Teresa's buoyant laughter. Of course, the more the aide tried to hush her, the more she laughed. The music, clicking cameras with flashes, long speeches, and the huge crowd, had completely saturated Teresa's senses at this point. The aide was not amused; neither was I, as I watched helplessly from a distance. The pair finally got to the stage, thank goodness. "Congratulations Teresa!" the principal said as she extended her hand for a handshake.

Teresa flapped her hands and excitedly turned the other way, apparently unaware of the importance of that moment. The principal smiled with obvious understanding, and the aide took the certificate from the administrator's hand on my daughter's behalf.

When they walked down from the stage, I met them with my camera and asked Teresa to pose for her photo. Rather than pose for me to preserve this momentous occasion with a dignified picture, she turned away, still laughing uncontrollably. Yet, that was Teresa. Thinking about it in hindsight, I suppose I captured the moment accurately.

I had not stopped crying for joy since seeing the slide show, but when Teresa missed the principal's handshake and the hand-off of the certificate, and then did not pose for my snap shot, I cried even more, although this time, it was not for joy. An emotional day and event in and of itself, my own emotions were in a tumult. I was flooded with pride: Teresa had graduated alongside her peers in spite of her challenges. At the same time, I felt a deep sense of loss.

All around me I observed the day unfolding so much differently for other parents and their typical children. Across from us, parents milled around in the cramped space around the stage, waiting to catch a glimpse of their children as they stepped down from the stage. Each graduating child posed solemnly and cooperatively for a photo. Though happy and excited, they were in control. They smiled, hugged, and chatted with family members. Their parents hugged them back with unbridled affection.

Teresa did not lend herself to a hug and a kiss from me. She appeared oblivious of the significance of all that was happening around her. She was so over-stimulated that she could not control her goofiness. Did she really understand what the event meant? It was hard to figure out how much she really knew.

In that moment, I felt like her disability was cheating her out of so many aspects of a meaningful life. Autism cheated her out of a life beyond knowing how to spell and do math calculations. It cheated her out of a life that is born out of forming relationships and understanding social situations. It cheated her out of an awareness of the respect and decorum associated with an occasion such as her graduation ceremony. But, still, I had to remind myself to hold on to our blessings, for as bad as I thought our plight was, our situation could have been worse. Teresa is Teresa. She is who she was meant to be on this earth, and maybe that is just right for her, though it may not seem okay to those of us with a "normal" perception of human experience and culture.

Remarkably, I did not see any parent stare at us or look at us with disdain in their manner. They were too busy happily fussing around their children and taking in every moment pertaining to their children's accomplishments to care about the distraction we caused. In a way, that was a relief for me; because, I did not need to feel guilty about taking anything away from a very special day for the parents.

# Twenty-Three

## Amherst, Massachusetts
## 2002-2004

One of the behaviors often associated with people with autism spectrum disorder is fixation. Children with autism tend to focus on very limited interests; and, when they find an object or topic of interest, they throw all of their time and energy into it to the exclusion of everything else. Their interest becomes intense, even obsessive. They become fixated.

Over time, Teresa's fixations have shifted from one thing to another, but in eighth grade, her fixation was on celebrities. With increasing intensity as the years went by, she dedicated most of her free time to looking at, collecting, or organizing celebrity photos, to the exclusion of everything else she could possibly do for leisure. She cut the photos out of magazines or printed them from the Internet. She then arranged them in a beautifully decorated scrapbook.

She also read about celebrities and created numerous lists of famous people that she found on the Internet, TV, and magazines. Every day she hand-wrote new lists, many of which were mere repetitions of previous lists. She stored her numerous lists in a folder that she guarded closely against any person peeking at it.

What was amazing to me was the fact that she could name the music, TV show, or movie to which the celebrities on her list were connected. As a result of her knowledge of celebrity trivia, she became my "encyclopedia" of famous people. If I forgot a celebrity's name, or if there was a particular song for which I wished to know the singer, all I needed to do was ask Teresa.

Her lists were eclectic in nature, as they comprised a mixture of male and female newscasters, singers, TV stars, and movie stars. One list that she titled "Actors" included older stars like Harrison Ford, Sylvester Stallone, Tom Selleck, John Travolta, Tom Cruise, Dan Shafer, and Ted Koppel. Another list, titled "The Actress," had fifty-four female stars, handwritten with pencil on both sides of the paper. Some of the celebrities in the list included Celine Dion and Cyndi Lauper, both of whose songs had become her favorite to listen to.

As her interest in the rich and famous grew, she realized that she might as well collect the magazines whose covers they graced. Her next collections then included a plethora of magazines, such as *Redbook, Teen People, Good Housekeeping,* and *Time.* One of her sources for her collection was a website she found during an Internet search. This website sold old magazines featuring celebrities on their covers. Some of the magazines dated back to the eighties and nineties and featured some of her favorite celebrities when they were fledging actors. One magazine had a very young looking Travolta on the cover. My guess is that the picture must have been taken either before or right after the movie *Grease* was released. Enthralled, Teresa asked me to buy this magazine and many others like it.

Teresa spent time with her magazines by lining them up on our living room floor in an array of rows and columns, creating a mosaic carpet of colors and faces. One day, I walked into the living room and noticed that the entire floor was covered with magazines while she lounged back enjoying the view.

Just like she did with her actor lists and celebrity scrapbook, she kept her magazines under close watch. No one was allowed to touch or even go near them. If anyone of us went near them, she would shove us aside and say, "Go away!"

During this time, she began collecting the CDs of her favorite sing-ers. After she collected the first few CDs, it occurred to her that DVDs and VHS videos featuring celebrities in films might also be a good idea, so she started contemplating the collection of those as well. At times, I felt like I was living in Hollywood as glamorous faces popped out in the most unusual places around our home.

At a point in time, her total personal collection of CDs, DVDs, and VHS videos surpassed the combined total of everyone else in the family. At first, she stacked them in shelves and drawers in her bedroom but when she ran out of drawers and shelves, she took over her sister's draw-ers and shelves; and when those got full, she used up the shelves in the family room.

Teresa's new interest in celebrities and collecting CDs, VHS videos, and DVDs was, nonetheless, a welcome turn of events. This was because her previous fixation was on baby dolls. By request, she received numer-ous baby dolls for Christmas and birthdays even in her teens. If not for her disability, she may have chosen to become a teacher when she grew up. This was because there was nothing that thrilled her more than play-ing school with her dolls. She played the "strict" teacher and her poor dolls were the pupils in an imaginary classroom.

She lined up the dolls facing her, and gave them instruction using an authoritative voice. For instance, she would say to them, "sit!" or "stand up!" Then she would attempt to teach them their ABCs by having them repeat the alphabets after her. Of course, the dolls are stone silent star-ing at her. But she kept teaching on. Then she would shuffle their posi-tion in line and continue to talk to them or give them orders.

On occasions I joined her at play. On one particular day when I joined her class as a pupil, she got a kick out of it when she gave me my instruction and I obeyed. She commanded me to "sit!", and I did, pre-tending to be meek like a student. Then she said "stand!" and I stood. She laughed so hard she almost passed out. Other than the sheer joy of spending time with her at play, I welcomed these moments with her, because it gave us opportunities to interact in meaningful ways.

Interestingly, when she turned twelve, she still requested baby dolls for Christmas and her birthday, even though I suggested age-appropriate alternative gifts to her. She not only requested baby dolls, she wanted their accessories too, like doll strollers, bottles, and diapers. She still played with them like kindergarten children did. It bothered me that at age twelve, items on her birthday and Christmas lists still included dolls and accessories for preschool-aged children such as *Baby Alive, Fisher Price New Born, Laugh and Giggles,* and *Barbie dollhouse.*

Naturally, I did not like seeing her play with dolls meant for toddlers and pre-school kids at her age, but I wasn't sure whether to continue to buy the dolls to keep her happy, or to stop in spite of her requests.

As I reflected on what to do, I recalled a debate that my graduate class at Xavier University had engaged in about this issue. The course was titled "Current Issues in Special Education," and the topic we discussed on this particular day centered on what a parent should do when a teenage child with a severe disability still wants to play with "baby stuff." My professor's position was that once children with severe disabilities passed childhood and were in their teens, parents should stop buying them children's toys, even if they asked for them.

On the other side of the debate, some of my fellow students argued the point that the teens with severe cognitive disabilities were still kids at heart, in spite of their chronological age and physical appearance. Would it not make sense to respond to their childlike needs, since that was where they were developmentally? After all, they were virtually kids in teen or adult bodies.

The professor had insisted that parents should not continue to buy kids' toys for them. She explained that this group of children were better off trained or weaned off such childhood wants, because it was unlikely they would do that naturally. She said if they were not deliberately weaned off, they could be twenty-five years old and still want to play with a Barbie. For that reason, she was of the opinion that parents should be proactive in seeing that those childlike toys were replaced with more age-appropriate toys or interests.

By the end of the discussion, I concluded that the professor's argument made sense. Therefore, when I was faced with Teresa's situation, I took the professor's advice and decided to wean her off baby dolls. However, I held off for two years until she turned fourteen before I made the move. I felt she was ready for the transition at this age, because she had started to show interest in collecting celebrity photographs, though she did not yet request them for Christmas or birthday gifts.

It was during the Christmas season of her fourteenth year that I initially made the move. First, I decided to have a talk with her about the dolls. I explained to her that she was now a big girl in middle school and that baby dolls were not for middle school girls. She did not buy my suggestion and insisted on her baby dolls for Christmas. Her Christmas list had three baby dolls on it. I yielded to her wish because I did not want to ruin her Christmas, but I gently reminded her that big girls did not buy "baby toys" and left it at that.

The following Christmas, when she was fifteen years old, she asked for only one doll. The other items on her list were CDs and videos. She got her wish, but I gently reminded her again that big girls did not buy "baby toys."

Finally, the year after that, when she turned sixteen years old, she did not ask for any dolls. She gave me a list of DVDs, CDs, and videos, and I could not be happier!

Apparently, my message had gradually seeped in and she had found a better replacement for her baby toys. Even though it took till age sixteen, I was glad she gave up her dolls voluntarily and I never had to ruin a Christmas for her. She held on to the old baby dolls though, refusing to give them up for donation; however, that was just fine with me. We had made progress.

It was not until she was about twenty-seven that she gave up her dolls and accessories. I was surprised one Saturday morning in the spring of 2015, in Houston, just before her twenty-seventh birthday, when she dragged her box of dolls to my room and woke me up saying, "Mom, go to Goodwill." "Oh! Do you want to give your dolls to Goodwill?" I asked.

"Yes." She said. And I said "Great! Ok, Goodwill next Saturday." And that was how the issue of dolls came to a close.

She had been organizing and re-organizing her closet for some time, and no matter how much she re-arranged it, she could not fit all of her belongings the way she wanted them: neat and tidy. So she figured that some things had to go, and the dolls were the first ones. I was happy she made the decision herself and in the process learned a valuable life lesson, which is to let go of things that are no more useful to you. She mentioned Goodwill, because I often took her with me whenever I made donations to the Goodwill charity store.

By this time I understood that fixation is simply part of the territory that comes with an ASD child. At least I could see that Teresa's fixations would grow and change, albeit slowly, which, when one thinks about it, is quite a "normal" human way to be. And, for the next several years we found the smiling flawless faces of celebrities instead of crying dolls around the house.

On my part, I made a point of embracing my child's "quirks" and enjoying them with her. Her fixations were part of who she was, and I accepted them. I really did savor the times I spent with her viewing celebrity photos in magazines. I used the time to engage her in small conversations in an attempt to practice her speech skills. But who knew what the next fixation would bring?

# Twenty-Four

## Amherst, Massachusetts
## 2001–2003

Teresa started at Amherst-Pelham Regional Middle School in the fall of 2001. During her seventh and eighth grade years she received inclusive instruction in a variety of subjects: science, social studies, home economics, art, and music. Her personal aide went with her to the inclusive classes where the aide and teacher modified assignments to her level. Teresa was taught reading, writing, and math in the special education resource classroom, and occupational therapy and speech therapy sessions continued as before. Middle school provided Teresa with a wealth of educational experiences, which the following entries from her "school-to-home" notebook will illustrate.

> *9/10/01 Monday*
> *Today we did some art projects after lunch. We then had English where we did some writing, reading, and comprehension worksheets. I think Teresa will have swimming 2 days a week, on Wed. and Thurs., so she will need her swimsuit and a towel. She had a really good day today! I hope you have a good night!*
> *AIDE*

*9/12/01 Wednesday*

*Teresa had a good morning. In advisory and social studies, the class had discussions about yesterday's events in NYC and Washington, DC (9/11 Twin Towers bombing). I was not sure how you handled it with Teresa or if you wanted it discussed at all. I simply asked Teresa if she knew what happened in NYC. She said there was smoke, so I left it at that. In English, we talked about music and instruments. She then had speech and then tech. ed. She then went to swimming! She was excited about being able to swim. We are still working on our plant samples in science. I hope you have a great night!*
*AIDE*

*9/13/01 Thursday*

*Tomorrow we are going to the Big E for a field trip. Teresa will need $8 to get in and some spending money for snacks or maybe some inexpensive shopping. I hope you have a good night!*
*AIDE*

*9/17/01 Monday*

*We started folding paper cranes in advisory this morning. The school wants to have a total of a thousand paper cranes to help with peace and healing for the events that happened Tuesday (9/11 in New York). Today, we collected more plant samples from outside for science.*
*AIDE*

*9/20/01 Thursday*

*We ran the school store for the first time today. We will be doing that every week. We finished our weeds and flowers samples. We are now making a table of contents and title page. I think we will be collecting samples for leaves starting next week. Have a good night!*
*AIDE*

*9/21/01 Friday*

    *Teresa had a great day bowling! It took her a little while to get into it, but then she loved it. We then had lunch at school. She had a really good day! Have a great weekend!*

*AIDE*


*9/24/01 Monday*

    *Today, Teresa finished her weeds and wild flowers packet. We are going to start on leaves next week. We are also working on parts of a cell. This part of the curriculum will be adapted. I'm going to talk to Kathryn about finding some reading and questions that Teresa will be able to understand easier. This week, we are doing art instead of wood tech. In social studies, we talked about longitude and latitude and found places in an atlas. She had a really good time in art! She talked about a picture that was up on the board. We will be starting the first project tomorrow. She had a wonderful day!!! I hope you have a good night!*

*AIDE*


*9/26/01 Wednesday*

    *In social studies, we are revising the Valley Almanac. Teresa has to make a "publishable" page. The page is focused on one group, town, or issue in the Pioneer Valley. We were going to do either maple sugar houses in the area or pumpkin farms. If you would like to read more about it, there is a yellow page in Teresa's notebook.*

*AIDE*


*9/27/01 Thursday*

    *Teresa had a really good day. In science, we are drawing a diagram of a plant cell. In social studies, we found pumpkin farms all around the Pioneer Valley. We will be getting a map and marking the farms in the different towns. Teresa painted in art class. I was trying to work with her on slowing down and taking her time. We also ran the school store today. Tomorrow we will be going to Atkins Farm for our field trip. If you*

*would like to send in some money for Teresa to get a small snack there, that would be great! Have a great night!!*
*AIDE*

The aide's frequent feedback on my daughter's exposure to a vast academic experience was very much appreciated. It made me feel like I was part of the school team, collaborating together to help my child's progress. My child was also trying hard, responding relatively well to positive behavior incentives in school to maintain appropriate behavior. She was rewarded with free time on the computer, snacks, listening to music, or watching a favorite video when she showed acceptable behavior. Unacceptable behavior was met with loss of those privileges or time-out.

At home, we continued to use the token system of positive behavior management to manage Teresa's behavior; at the end of each week she traded in her earned stickers for a meal from McDonald's.

Sadly, though the positive behavior reward systems and the various SID interventions used at home and in school were effective to some measure, the effectiveness was inconsistent and not far reaching. My child continued to struggle with inattentiveness, lack of focus, hyperactivity, restlessness, anxiety, crying for no apparent reason, and difficulty following directions.

She also battled insomnia, (common among children with autism) which got worse as she grew older. Lack of adequate sleep caused tiredness, which induced stress and increased her anxiety. Before long, heightened stress began to manifest in aggressive manners at home. For example, she would hit and throw things when she got frustrated over something.

Though I did not like her actions, I felt empathy for her. Like many other children with autism, she was dealing with multiple issues at the same time and there was no way of knowing exactly which issue was causing what. The impact of the brain dysfunction of autism, the impact of the sensory integration disorder, and the chronic insomnia all combined to make life difficult for my child. Though she wanted to earn her stickers and treats, her willpower was no match for the underlying biological causes of her symptoms.

In school these problems translated into incomplete assignments, loss of instruction, and the inability to maintain full presence of mind in the classroom. But more importantly, her symptoms were robbing her of her daily joy.

The situation caused us to once again confront a decision that many parents of children with autism often face at one time or the other: to medicate or not to medicate. We struggled with that decision during the time our child presented with behavioral difficulties.

Dr. Light's decision not to medicate Teresa in St. Louis caused us reason to pause, but what eventually convinced us to try medication was that we wanted our child to live a decent and productive life when she grew into adulthood. We reckoned that these early, formal educational years were fundamental in laying down the foundation for acquisition of lifelong skills, and we did not want the opportunity to slip away. We did not want her to miss her education. So, if medication was what we needed to place her behavior under control so that she could be educated and reach her full potential and thereby maximize her chances of living a productive adult life in the future, then that was what we had to do.

Working closely with her pediatric neurologist, and after trying a couple of different medicines, we finally found one that met our child's needs during her eighth grade year. The turnaround after medication was very significant; her behavior became manageable and under control. The medicine helped my child to maintain focus during instruction and enabled her to complete her school assignments without resistance. Now able to sleep well throughout the night, she was energized and attentive. She began to take her school work seriously and learned a lot more and faster than she had previously. She got her joy back too. She smiled and laughed more. It was as if everything fell in place.

What might work for one child might not work for another; so, I refrain from recommending any particular medicines as it is best to work closely with the child's doctor to find the best match if indeed a parent decides to try medication. My only recommendation is that if a parent wishes to explore medical treatments the parent should consult with a pediatric neurologist who specializes in autism or related disabilities, since these professionals tend to be well informed about medications for people with ASD.

I also think that medication should not be the first option. Positive behavior management systems do work successfully for some children with autism when used consistently and done in such a way that one or two behaviors are targeted at a time.

However, if behavior management systems alone do not work and if a parent wishes to add medication, then it will be best to consult with a specializing doctor. Regarding Teresa, it was a combination of positive behavior management systems and medicine that proved effective.

In eighth grade there were a variety of academic highlights that illustrated the degree to which Teresa's skills and maturity were developing. In math class she continued to learn the functional use of money by assisting in selling and keeping the books at the school store. She appeared to enjoy this real world application of her learning and the new sense of responsibility.

She also mastered the ability to add and subtract multiple digit numbers with regrouping, and she learned her multiplication tables, including multiplying by 0s, 1s, 2s, 3s, 5s, and 10s. She was introduced to division and fractions, though she did not gain mastery of them until she got into high school.

During a social studies project, Teresa got an opportunity to share her Nigerian culture and traditions with her peers. She shared the recipe of our family's all-time favorite dish of tomato stew and chicken, served with white rice and fried plantains (*Dodo*). She showed the class a Nigerian cookbook containing a variety of Nigerian recipes including main dishes, soups, and snacks. During her presentation, her classmates were enthralled by her outfit, which was a blue embroidered Nigerian kaftan, complete with a matching head wrap. (A kaftan is a loose and long dress with long, wide sleeves, commonly worn by women in Nigeria.)

In her science class she was paired with a non-disabled peer for a cooperative project. Though she did not understand a lot of the details of the project, she understood her role during the presentation, which was to hold their poster up while her partner explained their project. She was able, as well, to capitalize on her strength as a visual artist when she helped to decorate the poster. I was told that she did a marvelous job and that she exhibited an air of accomplishment at the end of the project. I was proud of her courage to stand up in front of a big class and not be intimidated.

During another science project, her aide described how, days before the presentation, Teresa practiced her PowerPoint slides over and over again. On the day of the presentation, she stood up confidently and gave her solo "lecture," which consisted of three memorized sentences about her topic.

Although Teresa may not have understood every fact, skill, or detail taught during her various middle school classes, the literacy skills she eventually acquired were a result of the varied, intense academic exposure that those classes afforded her over time. The exposure stimulated her intellect and caused her to learn and understand much more information than she would otherwise have had without the exposure.

Also, the opportunity to mingle with typically developing peers continued to provide role modeling and motivation for my daughter. It was, therefore, no surprise that she made the honor roll based on her individualized and modified curriculum. As a school tradition, the names of all honor roll students were published in the town's local newspaper. When Teresa saw her name in the newspaper she smiled with pride.

Her social growth was even more remarkable than her continued academic and intellectual growth. My young teenager was becoming popular within her peer group. In eighth grade, she had a group of girls that had befriended her and supported her. They walked to all of their classes together, and they were very good with helping her complete her assignments. Teresa liked these girls and felt comfortable in their midst. My daughter finally felt a sense of belonging.

The fact that she had a severe disability, yet was able to progress academically and socially endeared her to the school community. Almost everyone—students, teachers, and staff—knew her name and wanted to talk to her whenever they saw her. She also knew all their names and even their middle names! This was not at all a surprise to me, because along with celebrity photos and DVDs, she had also developed an enduring fixation for names and birthdays.

Whenever Teresa met someone for the first time, she made a point of asking the person his or her first, middle, and last name; then she asked for the person's birthday. The next time she saw that person, no matter how long since the first meeting, she would remember that person's full name and birthday.

Her ability to remember names was extraordinary. One day I found an old class photo of Teresa when she was in pre-school in Bayside, New York. There were six children and three adults in the picture. I asked Teresa if she remembered the names of the people in the photo. She looked at the picture for a moment and as I pointed to each person, she called out the names of every single person in that picture. This was nine years after pre-school, and she had not seen the photo since then. I did not ask her for the birthdays of those kids, but I bet she could have told me.

Her desire to know everyone's name and birthday was without boundaries. When we went to the mall she approached anybody that caught her interest and asked for the person's first name, middle name, last name, and birthday, in that order.

The reaction of some of her "fixation victims" was interesting to watch. Some people expressed wonder or surprise. Others looked suspicious. Sadly, most people had no reaction whatsoever; they simply ignored her and walked on. On occasion, people looked at me with expressions of curiosity. In response, I usually apologized and explained to them that she was a child with autism who was fixated on names and birthdays and that she meant no harm.

Senior citizens were the only ones who consistently welcomed Teresa's questionings. Many actually relished her attention and stopped to answer her questions. They had no qualms about sharing birthdays and ages with a teenage stranger. It is not surprising that seniors respond to her. They are usually retired, or lonely and seeking company and generally wiser and more understanding of disabilities.

Teresa's unusual talent with names did not go unnoticed at her school. At the end of eighth grade, she received the vote for "Most likely to remember your middle name!"

# Twenty-Five

## Amherst, Massachusetts
## 2003

While dedicated educators at school were doing their part to teach academics, speech, and social skills to Teresa, I was preoccupied with self-care instruction at home. Although she was a teenager, Teresa still had the same needs as a young child and, therefore, relied heavily on me for her daily care. One important life skill that took her a long time to acquire was bathing on her own. I had given her showers from the day she was born until she was fifteen years old.

It was at this age that she finally showed real readiness to bathe herself. Prior to that, she neither showed an interest to learn, nor demonstrated an ability to acquire the skill naturally. Whenever I left her by herself in the shower, she came out with half of her body still untouched by water or soap. Part of Teresa's resistance to learning how to self-bathe may have been due to her sensory integration issues, but I was not absolutely sure.

In any case, when she showed readiness to learn, I embarked on a training that was deliberate, meticulous, and elaborate. My goal for her was to be able to clean all parts of her body using soap and a sponge.

I tapped on Teresa's strength, which was the ability to learn quickly through the use of logical sequence and a sense of order. She could not learn when things were random, spontaneous, out of order, disorganized, or abstract.

I started Teresa's training during the summer months following her eighth grade year. In order to accomplish my goal, I utilized my professional teaching skills. Before the core of the training began, I did some preliminary preparation and pre-teaching. I ensured that soap, shampoo, sponge, and her towel were within reach in the shower area. Then, I broke the task of bathing into smaller steps.

First, I taught her to find the right water temperature in the shower by slowly turning the shower knob counter-clockwise, a task that turned out to be the easiest for her. Next, I taught her to associate her body parts with numbers. For example, the whole length of her left hand, and arm, including her left armpit, was 1. Her right hand, and arm, including the right armpit, was 2. Her neck and shoulder were 3. The general area around her chest, tummy, and waist (front and back) was 4. The left and right legs were 5 and 6, respectively. Her face and hair were 7 and 8, respectively. Numbering her body parts was necessary in order to give her a sense of order in carrying out the task of scrubbing with her sponge. After that, I taught her to lather her sponge with soap.

These preliminaries paved the way for the core of the training. First, I modeled how she should bathe. When I bathed Teresa, I scrubbed her body in order from 1 to 8. I simultaneously drew her attention to the number order so that she could make the connection and develop a system to follow. After about a week of modeling, we jointly did the scrubbing and rinsing. She was responsible to wash numbers 1-4 while I washed numbers 5-8. After two weeks she was given the responsibility to bathe herself fully, though with close guidance from me. Whenever she missed a step, I reminded her to go back. This guided practice took the longest time, but it was worth the time. Throughout the process, I frequently praised her for doing a good job.

Finally, eight weeks after the training started, Teresa was ready to bathe herself independently with occasional supervision from me. The first time it dawned on her that she had actually bathed independently and that she was clean all over, her pride was evident. From then on, each time she came out of the shower, she hurried to me with a beaming smile to tell me that she bathed herself. I always told her I was proud of her. I continued to minimally supervise Teresa during showers and give reminders here and there until the end of ninth grade. By tenth grade, my daughter did not need any more supervision. She has been bathing herself clean ever since.

To families who do not have children with autism or other forms of serious developmental disabilities, this need to place such focused training on something as routine as bathing may sound odd; however, those living with developmentally disabled children can relate. It is quite common to have to instruct teenage or adult children to shower or bathe. This is our reality. We cannot take these sorts of daily life skills for granted. I consider myself lucky that Teresa responded well to my training. Many teenagers and adults with developmental disabilities continue to rely on others for their daily cleaning rituals. It's hard to imagine the sense of independence that simply taking a shower can foster in a person with disabilities. I was so happy for my child that she gained this small responsibility.

# Twenty-Six

## Amherst, Massachusetts
## 2004

In her freshman year at Amherst Regional High School, which began in the fall of 2003, Teresa was placed in a "Life Skills Classroom", where she received instruction in functional academic skills. Functional academic skills are designed to help students with disabilities prepare for an independent or semi-independent adult life.

Life skills or functional academic instruction involves several key skills that most adults take for granted, such as choosing a restaurant, reading road signs, reading directions, crossing streets at cross walks, and recognizing important symbols such as bathroom and exit signs. Other functional academic skills include following a schedule and the ability to count and use money in realistic scenarios like making a budget, paying bills, cashing checks, and buying groceries. Students are also taught to understand the use of a calendar; to tell time; and to measure length, weight, and volume in practical ways.

Thanks to her special education teacher, Mr. Dave Stevens, Teresa made encouraging gains in functional academics. One of the ways he accomplished these strides was to have Teresa continue to maintain money skills by working at the school's coffee shop. With close supervision, Teresa worked there every other week and earned $5 a week. From training on the use of clocks and calendars, my child knew which days to work and reported to the store promptly at her designated time. With assistance from her aide, she gained experience receiving and counting money, making change, and conducting customer interactions. Teresa's coffee shop "job" provided a way for her to experience community beyond being a student in a classroom.

Alongside these practical needs, not surprisingly, reading is also considered an essential life skill and was a strong focus during Teresa's freshman year. One of her reading goals was to read more fluently with adequate pacing and correct pronunciation. In order to model fluent reading, as well as to expose Teresa and her peers to various human experiences and broader knowledge, Ms. White, a special education English teacher, often read aloud to Teresa's class. She read books from different literary genres, including tall tales, short stories, poetry, vignettes, and abridged Shakespearian plays.

The class even performed a short, modified skit of *Romeo and Juliet* (with a happy ending), where Teresa played the role of Juliet and a student in a wheelchair was cast as Romeo. The players read from their short, modified scripts while receiving prompts from their aides who sat close by.

Undaunted by the severe language and cognitive limitations of her students, Ms. White tried her best to make instruction fun and relevant to real life. She gained the students' attention and interest by modifying instruction to their level of understanding, by chunking their class work into smaller segments, by allowing as much time as they needed to complete their assignments, and by working with the students one-on-one.

The efforts of Ms. White and Mr. Stevens yielded positive results. In Teresa's end of semester progress report, her teachers summarized her strengths: "very organized, has a strong capacity to sequence or follow a given order, follows through when tasks are broken into small steps, works well with schedules, pays strong attention to tasks that she is interested in, and has a motivation to learn."

These words were like music to my ears. I could tell that my child was growing up. She still had a number of skills to work on, though. Among them were socialization skills, the ability to sustain conversation, and, in particular, initiating dialogue with peers.

Other literacy skills that needed improvement were writing grammatically correct sentences, use of correct grammar in speech, vocabulary development, and proofreading her writing. But, all in all, I was happy with her progress in academics and life skills during her first year of high school.

The most significant experiences for Teresa, however, were the ones connected with making art. Teresa's sense of sight is highly attuned. She has always loved pretty, bright colors. From a young age, she possessed the uncanny ability to match colors and was a pro at picking out matching clothes and socks to wear.

Her new aide Suzie, coincidentally, had a passion for art and had always wanted to work with autistic children who liked art. When I mentioned that Teresa had a strong artistic inclination, Suzie jumped into action.

To encourage and develop Teresa's artistic ability, Suzie, at my request, enrolled Teresa in an elective art class. Suzie nurtured Teresa's talent by finding creative projects for her; and, in return, Teresa responded with great interest when doing all of her art assignments.

In her first major art project Teresa used linoleum block (also called Linocut) to create an abstract geometric-style portrait. French artist Jean Metzinger made this approach popular. Suzie explained to me that the task of creating an abstract geometric portrait using a linoleum block involves painstakingly carving the intricate portrait on the linoleum block to make a stamp of the portrait. When the portrait stamp is made, it is printed out on paper.

I have to admit that I do not know a lot about art. So I relied on Suzie to explain Teresa's projects to me. Sometimes even with her explanation, I still did not get it. I can say with certainty that Teresa did not get her artistic affinity from me.

My child's impressive finished portrait was reproduced on a variety of colored papers. The surprise for her teachers and me was not so much the fine quality of her creation, but rather the tenacity and patience Teresa displayed during the creative process.

As word spread about the Jean Metzinger geometric portrait, many members of her school's staff became interested and placed orders to buy copies; so, Suzie printed more copies and framed all of them. She then asked Teresa to sign her autograph on every single copy, making each print special.

Seeing the enthusiastic interest from the school community, Mr. Stevens suggested that copies of the portrait be sold at the school's annual Christmas crafts fair. Suzie printed more copies, and Teresa autographed all of them. Copies of Teresa's framed art were then displayed in a prime spot at the entrance to the fair. The proceeds from the sales were donated to Teresa's art class to help toward the purchase of art supplies. Some money was also donated to Teresa's Best Buddies club to help fund their activities. Teresa received some pocket money as well for her efforts. It was a wonderful experience for her, and her popularity within the community soared.

During the second semester, Suzie helped Teresa with her second major project, which was painting a hibiscus flower utilizing the techniques of Georgia O'Keefe. O'Keefe is a well-known American painter who revolutionized the tradition of flower painting in the 1920s by painting large, oversized flowers and focusing on the details of the inner parts of the flowers.

Teresa reproduced O'Keefe's famous hibiscus flower by using a natural red color to paint the flower, and then contrasting numerous other shades of red against each other. In typical O'Keefe fashion, Teresa made the inside and center of the flower the focal point of the painting, almost taking up the entire canvas. Consequently, the shape and inside of the flower was stretched out further than it would look in reality; this is what made the flower painting stand out.

Teresa's third major art project, completed in the third semester of ninth grade, was a pair of six-foot by two-foot wooden panels that replicated South African cultural wall paintings. The idea of the project came about through a locally organized exchange program wherein students from South Africa were hosted in the high school for a year. This group of African students had a club focused on celebrating South African culture, and they were organizing a fundraising event at the high school.

The organizers were looking for student artists to help with cultural decorations and paintings; and, Mr. Stevens thought it would be a great experience for Teresa, so he volunteered her. Teresa's painting for the club was adopted to be her major project for her art class that semester.

Of her own volition, Teresa spent most of the semester painting the South African cultural panels, with its multiple colors and intricate geometrical designs. In a note home one day, Suzie wrote:

> *Teresa did a lot of painting today! I have a hard time getting her to stop because she loves it so much! Also, she really enjoys socializing with the other students lately. It is wonderful to see.*

The finished painting was donated to the African culture club, and after the fundraising event it was showcased in the school library for a period of time. During this time, and during all of the time that she worked on her art projects, Teresa seemed to enjoy the limelight that came with the recognition of her work. Another note from Suzie summarized Teresa's mood well:

> *I have never seen Teresa smile or laugh so much. She has been painting really well and her art teacher displayed a drawing she had done earlier on in the semester in the hallway. I am very excited about everything she and I are doing together.*

The Amherst community media also noticed Teresa's art projects, and she was consequently featured in two local Amherst newspapers, one of which was *The Amherst Bulletin*. In June 2004, the newspaper ran a story about the Third Annual Disability Awareness Week Fair hosted by the high school, and Teresa was one of few spotlighted student artists with disabilities. The article included photos of Teresa's Georgia O'Keefe Hibiscus painting and her Jean Metzinger portrait, both of which were displayed at the disability awareness fair. Her photograph and brief interview with the newspaper were also published.

I noticed that she did not react to the media attention in a typical way, which would be excitement and a sense of pride and achievement. Instead, when I showed the article to her she looked at it briefly, and just walked away with no expression on her face, as if to say, "big deal." I, on the other hand, was elated, and given the way she looked at me, I think she must have been wondering why.

The other Amherst paper that took interest in Teresa's artwork was *The Community Quarterly,* a family newsletter published by Community Resources for People with Autism. The paper published an article written by Suzie, Teresa's devoted school aide. In the article Suzie wrote a comprehensive story about Teresa, touching on her birth in Nigeria, her diagnosis with autism, our family, and our immigration to America. She also wrote about how she became Teresa's aide, noting the work and effort they had both put into Teresa's art projects. In this emotional and moving tribute to Teresa, Suzie noted that Teresa's artwork had helped to improve Teresa's life in significant ways.

Teresa's artistic accomplishments were officially recognized by her high school when she was presented with the award for Excellence in Foundations of Art in June 2004 during the annual end of year award ceremony. Not surprisingly, and to my embarrassment, she declined to attend the event, despite pleas from her teachers and me. Because this seemed to be a pattern, I felt like she did not like the spotlight. I picked up the certificate the next day.

All the accolades and recognition for her talent improved Teresa's self-confidence as well as her social interaction with teachers and classmates. Her persistence, tenacity, and total devotion to her art made me a very happy mom.

# Twenty-Seven

## Significant Danger

## Amherst, Massachusetts
## 2004

Like the saying goes, "Every rose has its thorn." If Teresa's educational experience in the Amherst schools was a rose, which I think it was, it certainly had its thorn. The thorn appeared when our path crossed that of another group of misguided students that rode the same special education bus as Teresa. Again, this ugly experience is not something I feel comfortable sharing, but at the same time, it was part of my daughter's educational experience as a child with a disability. I feel a responsibility to share the good and the not-so-good experiences, with the hope that enlightenment on the occurrence of such behaviors could move us towards solutions for behaviors such as these.

One afternoon I took Teresa to see her dentist at the Tufts University Dental Facility in Amherst. As we walked in, I noticed another mother and a skinny brown-haired boy of probably twelve or thirteen on the right side of the waiting room. The boy glanced at us briefly as we passed them on our way to sign in, and then he looked quickly away. I noticed he had his hands shoved deep in the pockets of his khaki shorts and was swinging his tennis shoes from a wooden chair.

While we waited for our turn to see the dentist, I heard him say to his mother that he rode the same bus as Teresa. He went on to tell his mom that he and his friends that rode the bus hated Teresa. When the mom asked him why, he said it was because Teresa liked talking to them, but they were not interested in talking to her. The whole time he spoke, his face was expressionless and his tone casual, as if he were talking about what he had for breakfast. He explained to his mom that they had asked Teresa to stop bothering them, but she would not stop.

Neither the mother nor the boy acknowledged that we were sitting just a couple of seats away. Then, with the same flat expression, he declared that he and the other boys had decided that they were going to kill Teresa. He said they planned to bring a tool onto the bus with which to hurt her. I listened with horror. Helpless to react, I sat momentarily frozen in my chair.

If the boy surprised me, the mother surprised me even more. She listened to her son's disturbing, hurtful plan with an equally emotionless demeanor. Her eyes remained focused on him the whole time he was speaking. Not once did she look our way to make eye contact with me. I wondered what was going on in her head as her son spilled out his deadly plan to her. Her body language and facial expression gave no clues.

When he finished, and, to my relief, his mother launched into a long speech about tolerance and respect for people. I felt a little more at ease, though I did not think she went far enough. Her reaction to something so serious appeared incongruently lackluster.

I finally found my wits and chimed in to defend my daughter, explaining to the young teen that Teresa was only talking to him and his friends because she just wanted to be their friend. She meant no harm.

After our long and intense counsel, the boy seemed remorseful and, in a gesture of contriteness, he brought out a collectible coin from his pocket and handed it to Teresa as a gift. It was a start, but did not ease my mind. And, though the mother had asked her boy for this apology, she never made an apology to me.

The following day, I talked to the bus driver about what the boy said and asked the driver if he knew of any such thing going on in the school bus. He did not give me a straight answer as to whether or not he had heard the boys threaten Teresa or plan an attack, but he told me that Teresa always sat quietly in the bus and never bothered anyone. He said that the group of students I was referring to was known to have serious behavioral problems and had gotten in trouble many times in school and inside school buses. They had actually been expelled from riding the regular school buses; hence, they currently rode the special education bus.

I was completely unnerved that boys with such a high level of misconduct hated Teresa so much that they had talked of planning to kill her. Knowing that they rode in the school bus with her daily and I never knew about their intentions caused me to confront my daughter's vulnerability in a way I had not had to before.

What if they had carried out their threat before fate intervened that day in the dentist's office? I felt a lot less trust in the world—I could no longer take for granted my child's safety while going about her ordinary activities. Every parent has to come to terms with this reality at some point, the reality that they cannot protect their child from malevolent intentions every minute of their lives. For a parent of a child with a disability, this moment of realization is quite alarming because children with ASD cannot express themselves properly as to report threats of this nature in a timely manner, and also because their extra-sensitivity to stimuli and lack of understanding of social situations can cause people to misunderstand them. I felt so lucky that those boys had not had a chance to physically harm her.

A couple of months after the incident, we moved to Texas to join my husband Dele, who had left a year prior to start a new job in Houston. Yet, I knew that simply moving away would not erase the fact that my child, like any other, was vulnerable in the world. Having ASD, she was even more so vulnerable because we live in a world where many people do not understand how to interact with children living with this form of developmental disability.

# Twenty-Eight

## MATURATION

## Houston, Texas
## 2004

**M**y children and I arrived at our new home in Seabrook, a suburb of Houston, in the summer of 2004. We enrolled Teresa at Clear Lake High School to begin tenth grade in the fall. (She had completed ninth grade at Amherst Regional High School.) Ovie would begin his freshman year at the University of Houston, while Elohor would return to Amherst in the fall to begin her junior year at the University of Massachusetts. I secured a job as a special education teacher at a local school district. We liked our new move and settled down quickly.

Teresa continued to take her medicine and her academic and behavioral progress continued steadily. In fact, her entire tenure at Clear Lake High School was remarkably uneventful as no behavior problems were reported; and, Teresa grew into a very organized, independent, mature, quiet, and respectful young woman. She took her responsibility for going to school very seriously and religiously kept her daily routine. She set her alarm for 5:50 a.m. every morning in order to shower and prepare herself for school on time, and then she eagerly climbed into her school bus every morning after she voluntarily hugged me.

Teresa did not like to miss a day of school; even when she did not feel well, she insisted on going. Whenever she had a doctor's appointment during school hours, she always asked to return to school after the appointment. Many children would have been happy to take the day off, but not her. As a result, I tried to schedule her appointments for very early in the morning or toward the end of the school day, in order to minimize her time away from school.

Teresa's program placement at Clear Lake was pretty much the same as that of her previous high school in Amherst, except for the fact that she did not have a personal aide at Clear Lake High. She was in the life skills program but received instruction for reading, writing, and math in the resource room from a special education teacher. Her elective classes were taken in an inclusive classroom with support from a general aide. Because of her level of independence, the service of a personal aide to guide her throughout the day was no longer necessary.

Periodically, her teachers sent home very good reports, not only about her great conduct, but also about her academic performance. She even became a model student for good behavior in her classroom. Her reading teacher told me that many students liked to sit by Teresa because she did not get in trouble with the teachers.

Also, although she would not volunteer to read in class, whenever the teacher called on her to read, she graciously took up the challenge and read aloud in class. A good oral reader, she was able to decode words at the fourth grade level, thus making her the top reader in her reading class that consisted mostly of struggling readers. Consequent to her relatively high oral reading ability, Teresa earned the respect and admiration of her classmates in reading class.

Her reading teacher was just as impressed as Teresa's peers. During the first parent-teacher conference, she could not say enough about Teresa: she was easy to work with, respectful to people, and compliant. Once she understood them, Teresa followed procedures and worked independently without needing to be redirected or reminded to focus. She maintained her excellent handwriting skills and her strong spelling ability. All of this was wonderful news. My joy was indescribable!

Teresa also demonstrated progress in her ability to answer "Wh" questions. When given a short and simple paragraph or story to read, she was now able to respond correctly to questions regarding *who, what, when,* and *where* in the story. She did better when the questions were given in a multiple-choice format as opposed to open-ended response.

Naturally, she still had some academic challenges. She had difficulty with reading comprehension when the text or story was long or when the content was complex. When she read from a long paragraph or a multi-paragraph text, the processing of the information became too much for her to handle, and she was unable to comprehend the meaning. Reading fluency continued to be a struggle. Although she decoded words well, she still had difficulty with adequate pacing, speed, smoothness, word pronunciation, and ease when reading out loud.

She also had great difficulty understanding the difference between fact and opinion. The ability to discriminate between the two concepts was in the state curriculum for her grade level. It was also one of her IEP objectives. But Teresa had such a hard time understanding the concepts that she often failed quizzes and tests on them.

Her teacher wrote several notes to me to say that Teresa always tried very hard but still came up short. She had been accommodated with extra time to process the materials and given one-on-one help but to no avail. However, I understood the reason why my child was not getting it: she thinks in concrete terms, while distinguishing the difference between fact and opinion requires thinking in the abstract. Children with autism usually have a problem with abstract thinking.

When I thought about this, I visualized Teresa trying hard and getting frustrated, and I felt bad for her. I decided to end her fruitless struggle. I wrote to the teacher, explaining that the exposure to the curriculum was good, but there comes a time when we have to face the facts. I explained that there are going to be some aspects of the curriculum or IEP objectives that will remain abstract or difficult to comprehend for

Teresa, even with accommodations and modifications, and when we hit that place, we needed to recognize it and let it go.

I told the teacher that we had hit that place with the concepts of fact and opinion, and I advised her to discontinue pushing it and concentrate on other areas where the child could experience success. I recommended that the concepts be removed from her IEP objectives.

Unlike in reading comprehension, Teresa's math computation skills remained solid. She knew her multiplication tables and continued to be able to add and subtract multiple digit numbers with regrouping (carrying). Her challenge lay in math reasoning. When math calculations were imbedded in a word problem, she had trouble understanding the problem because of the reading comprehension component. For example, a math word problem might read like this:

*John mowed the lawn for 7 days during the summer. If he was paid $10 each day he mowed the lawn, what was the total amount that John made over the summer?*

While Teresa could multiply 10 by 7 in isolation, she was unable to understand and essentially interpret this word problem.

The inability to understand math word problems aside, Teresa excelled in her ability to count large amounts of a combination of coins and bills. She made use of this skill at home. Whenever I had a large amount of money to count, she helped me count it accurately. Following her expertise in counting money, she became smarter with her cash and would no longer give it to me to hold. She bought a wallet for it, and started to save and watch it grow. She kept a close eye on her coins and bills, counting them periodically to ensure they were correct. When we went out shopping, I would ask her to pay for her own items with her money, but she would look at me with a facial expression that seemed to say, *seriously, are you kidding me?* She would insist that I pay with my money. When I told her that I did not have money, she would not let me off the hook.

"Use credit card, Mom," she would say.

Her frugality with money paid off quickly. At one point in time, after she saved cash gifts from her birthday, Christmas, and other sources, Teresa had a total of about $500.00 in her wallet. I barely had $20.00 in mine!

• • •

At home, it was a delight to see Teresa's transformation. She became a dutiful, responsible, and self-controlled young woman. Her chores, which she happily and willingly embraced, included washing dishes, cleaning the fridge, dusting furniture, vacuuming the carpet, making her bed, cleaning her room and bathroom, taking out the trash, and doing her own laundry.

Teresa was diligent about following through with plans and schedules. When it was her day to do dishes, for instance, she did so without needing reminders. She did not like dirty dishes in the sink for too long.

I trained her to do chores because I knew they were valuable skills to have for self-reliance. She was very receptive and actually took pride in her duties; the chores gave her a sense of accomplishment. Her dad and I showered her with praise in return for her contribution to the household.

In the evenings after she washed the dishes, she went straight to do her homework. Always wanting her homework done correctly, Teresa came to me when she needed help, frequently looking into my eyes for reassurance as she worked. I usually nodded to indicate a positive affirmation. One day, after I had helped her finish her reading comprehension homework, she looked up and asked me,

"Will I get a 100 percent?"

"Yes, you will score 100," I replied.

She beamed. Her question took me by surprise because I did not know that she cared that much about her grades. It was a sign that she had really grown up.

During the high school years, we got the most interaction with Teresa at dinner time, during which she liked to talk about her favorite celebrities. Notwithstanding her transformation described earlier, she still retained her autistic oddities and fixations, some of which remained a source of laughter for us. During supper, her fixation on celebrities caused her to ask us over and over again who our favorite celebrities were. She went around the table and asked each one of us about our favorite "girl singer," our favorite "boy singer," our favorite "girl movie star," our favorite "boy movie star," our favorite TV show, our favorite movie, etc. We also asked the same of her. She enjoyed listening to our varied responses to her questions.

Because she had asked us these questions many times previously, she pretty much knew the celebrities that everyone liked. So she played "gotcha!" whenever we gave an answer different from what we had given in the past. For instance one day, I mentioned Michelle Pfeiffer as my favorite "girl movie star." She looked at me straight in the eye and said "Julia Roberts!" Then I responded with a fake protest saying, "OK, both of them are now my favorites!" She chuckled with excitement.

Not to be outdone, I looked for an opportunity to do a gotcha on her too. Once, when she was responding to our questions, she said her favorite "girl singer" was Cyndi Lauper. That was true. Teresa actually had a collection of Lauper's songs. She mentioned her favorite "girl movie star" as Reese Witherspoon. She was again correct. She had Reese's *Legally Blonde* and *Sweet Home Alabama* on DVD. She was also correct when she mentioned *Knight Rider* as her favorite TV show and *Rocky* as her favorite movie. She had a collection of all the *Rocky* series.

I was beginning to lose hope that I would not catch her in a gotcha. She accurately mentioned Meredith Vieira of *Millionaire* as her favorite game show host and Bob Shafer of *60 Minutes* as her favorite newscaster. She watched both of their shows religiously. (Whether she understood what she watched was another matter.) But, when she mentioned Sylvester Stallone as her favorite "boy movie star," I got my gotcha moment. I said to her in typical gotcha fashion, "Harrison Ford!" She smiled with a quizzical look on her face that seemed to say, "*OK you got me there!*" Moments like this tickled her funny bone. Teresa inspired me to find joy in the little things, and that was special.

Teresa's fixation during the high school years extended beyond celebrities as she developed a new interest in the collection of Year Books. She asked to buy every year book for every year she was in high school. Because the yearbooks were not cheap, I grudgingly obliged her.

In addition to her personal collection of yearbooks, she took all of her siblings' middle school and high school yearbooks and made them hers. Her siblings did not particularly care for them, so they let her keep their Year Books. She kept her private collection of yearbooks under her watchful eyes, in a plastic bin close to her bed. Occasionally she brought them out and viewed them, studying the pictures, faces, and names of all the students. You could see her sense of delight as she slowly turned the pages and savored the moment with a smile.

Due to the fact that she could not get enough of Year Books, she browsed for Year Books every Saturday at our local library, where she went weekly with Elohor. I did not even know that libraries kept a collection of Year Books from many years past until I saw Teresa in the section. She viewed the Year Books over and over again with renewed interest and vigor each time. Sadly for her, the Year Books in the library were in the "Not to be borrowed" list. I say for good reasons because for Teresa, they would have been painful to return.

● ● ●

By virtue of her autistic nature, Teresa liked a sense of order; so, I sometimes felt bad for her, because our family was not always consistent and orderly in the way we went about our daily lives. If our differences frustrated her at times, she did not show it. She was calm, compliant, and gracious in trying to maintain her linear order amidst our ever changing and spontaneous ways.

Some days I would contemplate how far she had come, and it was hard to fight back my tears. My daughter had strengths for which she had earned deserved recognition at school and in the community. She had cultivated social relationships, friends even. She was independently carrying out daily routines and self-care. And, she was doing it all with graceful confidence.

# Twenty-Nine

## Houston, Texas
## 2005

One October day during her junior year at Clear Lake, Teresa brought home a flyer that she couldn't wait to give to me. In her typical clipped grammar, she spoke with urgency.

"Teresa go to party, Halloween party!" She still referred to herself in the third person.

I took the flyer from her and read it. It was an invitation to a Halloween party organized for students with disabilities by a nearby high school. The party was open to all special needs students in local middle and high schools. Because I was always looking for opportunities for her to socialize in positive environments, I agreed.

But first, we needed a Halloween costume. After a long and hard search, Teresa and I finally found a one-of-a-kind clown costume, which was an outrageous oversized jumpsuit of multiple colors. We purchased the costume from a very large, newly opened Halloween store. Teresa picked it out of a myriad of costumes and it cost me fifty dollars. At the time I thought it was too much money for a costume, but it proved to be worth it in the long run.

The middle section of the costume was white. The sleeves and attached jacket were black with yellow polka dots. The bottom part of the jumpsuit was green and black with diamond-shaped designs. An oversized ring about 3 feet in diameter was attached around the waist of the pants, exaggerating the bulkiness in the lower half of her body. An oversized tie, which was pink and black with diamond-shaped designs, was attached to the front neck of the jumpsuit. The outfit was topped off with matching oversized, fluffy hat. It was extraordinary to say the least!

I remember very well the first time Teresa wore the clown costume on the night of the Halloween party. After putting it on, Teresa looked in the mirror and burst into laughter. I laughed too, especially when I saw her walk around. She could not walk straight at first. It required a balancing act and took some practice, but she got it right after only a few minutes. You see, she learns quickly!

Getting into the car with the costume was an interesting scene! Let's just say it took some creativity. However, it helped that my vehicle was a roomy Toyota Sienna van. As we drove to the venue, I asked if she was excited. She said "yes", and then burst out laughing. I repeated my question again minutes later, and she laughed even louder. I kept her laughing until we got to the place.

The gymnasium of the school where the party was held was a merry environment. There were many chairs and tables laden with party food, such as pizza, cupcakes, chips, and chocolates, arranged in an inviting manner. There must have been up to one hundred students, both disabled and non-disabled. The non-disabled students were looking out for the disabled students, encouraging them to dance and join in the fun. The DJ played popular music like "The Macarena," "Thriller," and "The Electric Slide." The music was loud but pleasant, and parents and children alike danced joyfully.

At one point when all the dancers were moving in a circle, I saw a non-disabled student take Teresa's hands and guide her in the right direction that the circle was taking. Thrilled, she followed happily. At times, I joined in the dancing, letting loose like my daughter and joining the dance circle along with other parents. In addition to dancing, there were also numerous fun games and friendly competitions, and of course, all of the foods and sodas were free.

In the dance competition, an adorable girl with Down syndrome won. The girl loved to dance and could dance very well, continuously dancing without breaks. The only time she stopped dancing was when the DJ temporarily stopped the music to make announcements or to talk about a contest. Her father told me that all she wanted to do was dance.

Towards the end of the evening, Teresa won the best costume prize. Her outfit was so outlandish and unique that everyone loved it. I thought I got my money's worth for the costume when Teresa chose to continue to wear this same costume year after year for Halloween for the next four years. Even then, when she retired it, she would not let it go. It hung in her closet for many more years. During our spring-cleaning in March of 2015, she was bringing out clothes and other belongings she no longer cared for in order to free up space in her closet. Suddenly, and quite unexpectedly, she showed the clown costume to me.

"Mom, Goodwill?"

"Yes, Teresa, that can go to Goodwill now."

The next day, we donated the costume along with other unwanted items to a nearby Goodwill thrift shop.

Of all of Teresa's social events, the one that amazed me was the Buddy Idol singing contest. The Buddy Idol singing competition was organized by Teresa's club, Best Buddies. Best Buddies Club pairs people with disabilities together with their non-disabled peers in order to foster the development of meaningful friendship between the parties.

In the Buddy Idol singing contest, students with disabilities (with assistance from each of their non-disabled buddies) competed against each other by singing karaoke in a spontaneous performance. There were no prior selections of candidates. There were no rehearsals or practices. On that day, members of the club, their families, and friends gathered in the school gymnasium at around 4:00pm. The benches on one side of the gymnasium were packed with people. Teresa and I sat on the third bench up from the floor. We were sandwiched by two other families on either side of us. The air was filled with anticipation and excitement, though I had no idea that my daughter was going to make a spontaneous decision that would amaze me.

When the master of ceremony asked for volunteers to sing, to my surprise, Teresa held up her hand. She and other volunteers were then invited to the center of the school gym where the contest would take place.

*What is she going to sing?* I wondered. *I have never heard or seen her sing in public before.*

The contestants took turns and Teresa was the seventh in a line of about ten student competitors. When her name was called, she walked gingerly to the stand, and, with her buddy at her side, took the microphone and sang quite a rendition of "Lonely No More" by Rob Thomas. *How did she know the lyrics to that song? When did she learn it?* I was dumbfounded! The crowd cheered, and she won second place. I watched proudly as she basked happily in the ensuing attention. This moment was significant in her progress regarding social skills and non-verbal expressive ability. Whereas back in Amherst when she won the art award and at another time when she was featured in a newspaper article, she did not express any emotion, this time around, she was visibly happy to win second place. It was yet one more step forward. She was moving away from having a flat affect to a more typical emotional response.

Capitalizing on my daughter's growing interest in socializing with her peers, I signed her up for bowling at our local Special Olympics. She had become a very good bowler and loved the sport. She dedicatedly practiced bowling along with fellow Special Olympic athletes for many months preceding the local competition.

When the day of the main event arrived, the athletes were grouped according to their abilities. Teresa was placed in the group with the highest ability. The competition took place at a local bowling alley, where a large crowd of family members, friends, and bowling fans cheered for every athlete, irrespective of whether they knew him or her. Everyone was proud of the athletes for their bravery in participating, and I could tell the athletes felt a sense of accomplishment as well.

At the end of the competition, the officials named three winners with the highest scores from each ability group to win the bronze, silver, and gold medals. The winners were called one at a time to walk to the podium to receive their medals, as the crowd cheered.

Teresa's group was the last to be honored and when their turn came up, nobody could guess who the three medal winners would be. The announcer called the name of the third place winner to a round of applause; then the second place winner to another round of applause; then he abruptly stopped. Spectators were wondering why he stopped. He approached another staff member standing nearby and they talked for a little bit, both staring at the paper he was holding.

A few seconds after, the announcer returned. With apparent uncertainty in his voice, he announced, "The first place winner is Teresa Z...z...z.u...uma!" Apparently, as we later learned, the man was not sure how to pronounce my daughter's last name, but he wanted to get it right. At the end, it was still pronounced incorrectly, but it did not matter.

The applause in the room was deafening. As if in slow motion, my daughter got up and walked to the front of the hall to take her place in the line-up of winning athletes.

She wore a huge smile as she received her gold medal. She openly expressed her happiness at winning through her smiles and chuckles. It was a delight to watch.

In true Special Olympic spirit, every athlete who competed went home with an Olympic participation medal. At the end of the day, everyone was a winner.

Teresa's win qualified her to compete at the state level in Austin, Texas, but she declined the invitation. She did not want to leave Houston, and she was done with bowling.

After the long months of evening practices that caused her to miss her favorite TV shows at home, coupled with the loud crowd and the long waiting time involved in the sport, my child was ready to quit, and understandably so.

"Mom, no more bowling!" she said when we got home that day.

I nodded in agreement. She had given her best and succeeded. Now it was time for the next accomplishment.

# Thirty

## HIGH SCHOOL GRADUATION

## Houston, Texas
## 2009

The special education law, IDEA, provides an option for parents to leave children with developmental disabilities in school up to the age of 22. This meant that Teresa could stay an extra three years beyond her final year in high school if we so chose. Dele and I thought long and hard about this and then decided to take advantage of this provision. When she completed her senior year, instead of graduating, we sent her back for her first extra year.

During the first extra year, she continued to learn and work toward her individualized academic and vocational goals. On completion of the extra year, we waived graduation again and sent her back for her second extra year. Our plan was that she would go for a third extra year.

But shortly before she completed the second extra year, she came to me one day after dinner.

"Mom, when Teresa graduate high school and go college?" she asked in her typical grammatically flawed manner.

I was touched by her unexpected question. Apparently, she had seen her two older siblings graduate high school and go off to college, and so assumed she would be doing the same. Taken by surprise, I was not sure how to respond to her question, so I told her I would think about it.

The truth was that Dele and I did not know what she would do post high school, and we did not want her to stay home doing nothing. We wanted to buy time by having our daughter stay in school as long as the law allowed. The extra years would benefit our daughter by giving her more time to learn life skills in order to be better prepared for the real world. Specifically, we thought this opportunity would give Teresa more time to mature, and improve her reading comprehension and speech skills. Many other parents in our situation have embraced this option as well.

However, after Teresa's surprise question, it became clear to us that she was tired of going back to school. So one day, I sat her down and told her our plan.

"Teresa, you will graduate high school in May!"

She looked at me with surprise for a moment.

"No more high school for Teresa?"

I nodded in affirmation with a smile.

"Yay!" she yelled, jumping up and giving me a hug.

I realized at that moment how much it meant to her. Teresa did not go back for a third extra year. At 21 years old, she was finally set to graduate high school.

May of 2009 was a very happy day for our family. On the day of graduation, Teresa dressed up professionally in a black pair of pants and a yellow blouse, accessorized with silver earrings and necklace. She enthusiastically donned her graduation gown before we entered our car for the ride to the graduation ceremony.

The evening ceremony was held outdoors in the Veterans Memorial Stadium in League City, a neighboring town to Seabrook, where we resided. Soon after we arrived at the arena, Teresa joined her fellow graduating classmates in the area reserved for them in the middle of the ballpark. All the graduates sat in rows. Because her last name started with a Z, her seat was the last one in the last row.

She sat quietly and patiently as she watched all of the festivities around her. The day was very hot, and the long ceremony was comprised of many lengthy speeches, much of which she did not fully understand. But neither the heat nor the long speeches fazed Teresa, who kept her pleasant poise throughout the ceremony.

From the fringes where families and visitors sat, I cheered and shouted out her name every now and then to get her attention. Most parents did the same to their children, resulting in an unintentional shouting match between groups of parents and supporters; a competition carried out in a festive spirit.

Sometimes, Teresa looked my way and smiled when I yelled out her name. At other times, she did not turn her head, but rather looked straight ahead expressionless. I was not sure if she just decided to ignore me, because my yelling was beginning to embarrass her, or if perhaps she did not hear me; either way, I could not help myself and kept yelling out her name. The rest of my family kept their poise.

After what felt like an eternity, the time finally came for the graduates to receive their diplomas. Waiting for my daughter's name to be called was hard, because she was the last name on the list. Then the moment arrived, and my family heard "Teresa Zoma!" announced over the speaker.

The graduates got up and strode confidently past dozens of rows of chairs to the stage. Because Teresa was the last one to be honored, the whole stadium stood up and cheered for her. From the time she left her seat, I clapped my hands and repeatedly shouted her name until she reached the stage, but my shouts were drowned by the overwhelming ovation from the entire stadium.

She shook the hand of the principal and posed for a photographer's camera lens; quite a contrast from her sixth grade graduation (when her hyper-stimulation caused her to miss the principal's handshake and ignore the acceptance of her certificate, while she giggled out of control throughout the ceremony). This time around, after posing for a photo, my daughter walked a few steps to receive her certificate from another dignitary. Finally, she followed the line with the rest of her graduating class back to her seat, all the while maintaining poise and grace.

This time my daughter understood what a graduation meant as well as appropriate behavior to follow during a formal ceremony; and, she conducted herself with decorum. When the ceremony was over, a school aide helped my child find her way through the crowd to the sidelines to wait for us.

My family and I quickly made our way through the large crowd to meet her for a big hug. Over and over again I expressed my pride in her and she quietly nodded her head in response to my gushing compliments. After that, we took pictures with family and friends and went home to celebrate with food and refreshments. I was so thankful that our life seemed to have come full circle.

# Thirty-One

PROGNOSIS POST GRADUATION

## Houston, Texas
## 2009-2017

Teresa is not cured from autism. However, the speech and occupational therapies, the academic and behavioral interventions employed by the myriad of professionals that worked with her, and the medication have combined to rehabilitate her beyond my expectation.

I am particularly pleased with her progress in self-help and life skills. That she is able to function independently, safely, and appropriately in her daily life with minimal supervision is a huge success. She has a keen awareness of what is safe and what is not and follows rules religiously. She is able to groom and dress herself, prepare cold meals like sandwiches and salads, and can heat up foods in the microwave. She cleans, does laundry, and washes the dishes without being told. She knows how to entertain herself and can spend long productive hours on her own. In addition, she is responsible and respects others. Best of all, she is peaceful, content, and happy.

Teresa is also literate. She can read at the fourth grade level and write at the third grade level. Her math calculation skills are at the fourth grade level. She is highly skilled in computer technology, including the ability to type at a remarkable speed. When accompanied to the store, she can shop and pay for her items with the correct amount of money. She has enough language to communicate her needs and wants, as well as to make brief conversation with people she knows.

Although she may not attain the intellectual ability to attend college, earn a living, or get married and raise children, with her current skills, Teresa will be able to depend less on other people, enjoy life, and make meaningful contributions to society.

Currently, she attends a day program for adults with disabilities. Day programs are designed for adults with disabilities who no longer attend school. They provide a continuum of services appropriate for varying levels of abilities. The programs provide structure throughout the day for the clients and simultaneously attend to the clients' educational, social, communication, and life skills needs. We found a program that is just right for Teresa, and she enjoys going there daily. Parents looking for Day programs for their post-high school children can contact their state's Department of Aging and Disability.

During the next phase of our journey together, our family's greatest challenge will be in the area of communication. Teresa's ability to process verbal information is still slow, and making sense of a large amount of verbal information at once is difficult. To accommodate her, I talk slowly, relay smaller chunks of information, and allow her extra time to process what I am saying. I also edit out irrelevant words and limit my sentences or phrases to the bare minimum needed to deliver my message. For example, instead of saying, "Tomorrow, we will go to the doctor. You need a new prescription for your medication and you also need to do a fasting blood test, so do not eat breakfast," I will paraphrase by saying, "Tomorrow, doctor's appointment; you need new medicine and blood test. No breakfast. OK?"

When trying to express herself, Teresa sometimes struggles with word retrieval, even when she knows the word she is seeking. Because she has not fully developed the ease of spontaneous language, I provide her with pre-written scripts on note cards to read from whenever she is verbally having difficulty finding words or organizing a sentence.

The use of a pre-written script has helped a lot. For example, when we are at a fast food restaurant and she is being asked to make her order, she looks at her note card as a reminder of what she needs to say. If there are follow up questions from the server, Teresa has her notes to prompt her.

This expressive deficit makes extended dialogue tedious for her. It is hard for her to maintain a conversation for a long time, because she cannot keep up with the demands of forming new sentences spontaneously; so, she gives up.

The subtle complexity of the use of language makes it hard for Teresa to recall past events in detail and in proper sequence. This skill requires her not only to be able to use language spontaneously, but to also manipulate words and details during the process of remembering, while the listener is looking at her and processing the story.

For these reasons, her recall of past events comes out choppy. For example, if she were asked to tell what she did at, say, the amusement park earlier in the day, she would most likely respond with incomplete or disjointed information, and without clear order or details.

The way I accommodate this difficulty for her is by asking a series of short, direct questions instead of asking an open-ended general question. For example, rather than ask, "What did you do at the amusement park today?" I might ask several questions like:

"In the park did you go on a ride?"

"What was the name of the ride?"

"Did you go on another ride?"

"Did you eat?"

She can verbally provide accurate, simple answers to these kinds of specific questions.

Another language problem is that Teresa's grammatically incorrect sentences sometimes obscure her meaning. Whenever I am unable to understand what she is trying to say, I give her a notepad and pencil to write down her intent. Writing takes the pressure off having to construct spontaneous speech.

My daughter also continues to address herself in the third person most of the time. For example, if she is asked who had left the magazines on the table, she will respond by saying, "Teresa," instead of "me." I usually remind her to restate her answer, and she quickly corrects herself.

Teresa is also very literal in her language comprehension. Nuances, idioms, and figurative language are hard for her to understand. This is the case with most people with autism.

Those of us with normal language processing ability do all of these language tasks without even thinking. It's automatic. But, that is not the case for people like Teresa. In general, I consistently apply many strategies to support her communication efforts. Some effective accommodations are listed below.

- *Present important information slowly and deliberately on a one-on-one basis.*
- *Establish eye contact.*
- *Repeat information.*
- *Give short, precise, clear directions.*
- *Provide additional processing time.*
- *Diffuse anxiety, confusion, or reduce pressure over misunderstandings, by observing body language and adjusting language as needed.*
- *Provide encouragement and re-assurance.*
- *Frequently check for understanding.*
- *Use concrete language and avoid abstractions.*
- *Break tasks into small chunks.*
- *Model or employ visual representation of activities.*

• • •

When I think back on Teresa's struggle with language from her early childhood through high school, I imagine that during her early years the English language sounded to her like a string of meaningless sounds. Although she could recognize a few words out of the lot, they were hardly enough to construct useful meaning. What she perceived could be comparable to what the rest of us experience when we hear a foreign language for the first time. "It's Greek to me," we usually say. I am happy to report that today, in spite of her lingering communication shortcomings, the English language does not sound like Greek to her anymore.

Acquiring stronger language skills has opened up more opportunities for socializing and creating relationships for Teresa, and she has made very good progress; however, her autistic traits remain apparent. She tends to shun the busy happenings of the outside world, preferring to be alone in her room most of the time where she derives comfort and contentment in quietness and solitude. She often declines my suggestions to go sightseeing or to the movie theater. She sees no need to go to the crowded theater when she can watch DVDs at home.

Ever the foodie, she does love to eat out in restaurants when we celebrate birthdays; however, on a regular day or weekend, she prefers take-out. She goes shopping with me only because it affords her the opportunity to browse for DVDs and CDs, items that she still loves to collect. She no longer actively collects magazines, and she recently gave up all of her magazine collection to Goodwill.

When she is not out shopping for DVDs and CDS, Teresa's leisure activities are, for the most part, solitary, such as spending time on her computer, during which she enjoys viewing videos from YouTube. When she is not on her computer, she likes to watch TV or movies. She also loves to listen to music and play video games.

Though she does not like to get out regularly, she loves to take long walks with me on the weekends. She also makes bi-weekly trips to the local library with her big sister, Elohor, from where she borrows many

DVDs and books; most of the books Teresa checks out are about celebrities of course. No surprise there! She reads the books for leisure, although as far as understanding everything she reads, one cannot be exactly sure of the depth of her comprehension.

One of the best things about Teresa's overall growth and development is that she is able to be flexible when the occasion calls for it. She no longer gets upset or throws a fit whenever she does not have her way or when we run into situations that are different or that call for spontaneity. Generally, she politely goes with the flow of things. Her ability to be flexible and adapt to change is a testimony of how far she has come.

While she can be flexible, she continues to prefer things to be predictable and to follow the same daily routine. For instance, she wants to know what she will have for lunch and dinner a day or more ahead of time. Shortly after I serve dinner on a Monday, she will say to me, "Mom, what's for dinner Tuesday?" Most of the time I have no answer because I usually do not think that far ahead. I am more of a spontaneous person.

In order to make things easier for both of us, I make a meal schedule for the week and place it on a clipboard where she can access it at any time. She loves her food schedule and I love that I know what to cook each day and do not need to think about it anymore. Sometimes, her need for structure helps to simplify my own life!

My daughter's overall improvement is also apparent in the fact that she no longer shows serious symptoms of Sensory Integration Disorder (SID). The acute symptoms of SID gradually faded out by the end of her teen years. Today, at twenty-nine years old, she initiates and enjoys receiving hugs. She moisturizes her legs and hands by herself, and has no problem with the sound of running water. She tolerates being on the dentist's chair as much as anybody. Best of all, she is focused and attentive. If she suffers irritations from certain sounds or other environmental stimuli (she still does to a lesser degree), she appears to have better control of her reactions. Sometimes, she requests that I turn off the radio or TV when the sounds become irritating.

I thank God that we have made it this far. Looking back, I could not have imagined this level of transformation. When I think back to our experiences in New York and the tantrums Teresa threw; when I consider the fact that she could not make a complete sentence to communicate at nine years old and still relied heavily on pointing and gestures to communicate; when I think back to when she was twelve and I was elated, because she engaged her teacher in conversation for a brief moment by using a combination of phrases and a sentence; when I think about factors that inhibited her learning, like SID, insomnia, silly behaviors, agitations, anxiety, aggressive ways, and difficulty with focusing and paying attention in elementary and middle schools; I did not think she would turn around and become the mature, literate, responsible, controlled, self-reliant young woman that she is today. For that, I am eternally grateful.

If there is one thing to take away from our story, it is that there is always hope. Difficult challenges can change for the better if we keep trying. If one strategy does not work, we try another. We keep pushing and searching until we find a solution. We refuse to give up. Where we end up may not be exactly where we wanted to go; there may not be a cure, results may not be perfect or even what we imagined, but sometimes what emerges may be better than what we envisaged. There may sometimes be an unexpected outcome that is truly magical if we can perceive its value and appreciate it.

Inside a box of chocolates, we may never know what we're going to get; and, when we open it, we might discover a few chocolates that we may not care for. However, if we look closely, there might be a whole lot more that we may like, and when we discover those delicacies, we savor them with relish. We need only have faith that positive moments, humorous moments, surprising moments, and successful moments, large and small, will come. When those moments arrive, we embrace them with gratitude.

# Afterword

**M**any people have asked me about what they can do to help families who have children with autism spectrum disorder (ASD) or other developmental disabilities.

First, simply reaching out to families living with ASD is a great place to begin. It is okay to let them know that you are available to babysit, help out with groceries, run errands, or even take the siblings to a park. Young siblings of children with autism don't always receive the attention they deserve because the demands on their parents are overwhelming. I accepted numerous offers from a friend of mine in New York City to take Elohor and Ovie out when they were young. I appreciated her help very much.

If a family declines help, do not take it personally or give up on asking the next family, because every family's needs are different.

Another helpful way to respond to families such as ours is to volunteer time to causes that raise money for autism research or which promote awareness of the condition.

By far, the most important thing one can do is to support legislation that is geared toward improving the lives of people with ASD. Take time to call your legislators' offices to inform them of your support of disabilities laws. It is certainly not a waste of time to do so, because I know firsthand that those individual calls make a difference. Information on current and upcoming legislations relating to autism can be found on the Autism Society of America's website, www.autism-society.org, or the Autism Speaks website, www.autismspeaks.org.

People often forget that autism is a brain dysfunction; that means that the brain is not working as it should. As parents, teachers, service providers, and citizens, we must therefore continuously remind ourselves that most ASD behaviors are not the fault of the children or adults living with the condition. The behaviors are the result of the brain dysfunction over which those with ASD, especially children, have little or no control. They are doing their best with the hand that nature has dealt them.

I see too many children with autism who are punished in schools or removed from classes for misconducts that are associated with their condition. They lose a lot of learning time as a result. Eventually, they lag behind. They are usually blamed for their behavior and expected to snap out of it. These children deserve our empathy and patience. They are likely just as tired of their fits of temper or misbehaviors as the adults around them. We as a community should, therefore, be persistent in our search for solutions geared toward treatment and rehabilitation of these children.

The end goal for all in a community is to have all of our children (both disabled and non-disabled) reach their full potential and live productively and harmoniously with people around them. Partnership between parents, friends, family members, schools, and community organizations is paramount in pushing for legislations that make provisions for rehabilitative treatments, therapies, and teacher training in schools and Day centers.

Children with disabilities especially need valuable opportunities to mingle with typical (non-disabled) peers, because children with disabilities learn so much more from their typical peers than we will ever know. The time Teresa spent in her inclusive classrooms was tremendously important to her learning. As much as possible, parents and educators should seek ways to give inclusive experiences to children with developmental disabilities.

In addition, I highly recommend that families or friends of individuals with ASD join associations that advocate for people with autism. Such organizations provide an opportunity for those affected to interact with fellow members in the same situation, and they offer a great network of information and support.

Last but not the least, if one suspects something is not right with an infant or toddler, it is important to see a doctor as soon as possible. Early intervention treatment services for children ranging in age from birth to three years can greatly improve a child's development. The Individuals with Disabilities Education Act (IDEA) states that children under the age of three years (or thirty-six months) who are at risk of having developmental delays may be eligible for early intervention services in their respective states. A child does not need a diagnosis of ASD to receive needed services. One can find programs in any state for infants and toddlers with disabilities, from age birth through age five, by calling one's state's department of education.

Early intervention programs for children with autism are varied and different in approach. However, from my experience as a special needs educator, I think that a combination of the use of Applied Behavior Analysis (ABA) by a trained, licensed ABA therapist, coupled with intensive speech therapy by a licensed speech pathologist, and ample opportunities for the child to mingle with typically developing peers socially, will all work together to give the child a greater degree of recovery.

I use the term "degree of recovery," because all of my readings so far have indicated that there is no cure for ASD, and I have not personally seen any child who has been "cured" of autism, although a cure might exist. What I do know is that with the right combination of treatments (speech therapy, behavior management, and education), the extent of recovery can significantly increase. I also believe that the degree of the recovery will be dependent upon the severity of the condition, as the disorder can range from mild to severe.

Teresa's presence in my life reminds me that everything happens for a reason. Her birth gave me purpose and direction and inspired me to help children and families in our situation. I would not have chosen to be a special education teacher and an advocate for people with disabilities if not for Teresa. I feel great honor and immense privilege to walk in this path of service.

Because this book seeks to help young families living with autism, I would like to highlight once again the strategies that I used (and still use) for my daughter and which are very helpful in interacting with her. I hope others find them helpful as well.

- *Present important information slowly and deliberately on a one-on-one basis. If information were given to a group of people, your child included, do not always expect that the child will understand everything. Pull the child aside and repeat the information one-on-one.*
- *Establish eye contact.*
- *Be patient and repeat information as often as needed. Avoid saying "I told you five times already."*
- *Give short, precise, and clear directions.*
- *Provide additional processing time.*
- *Diffuse anxiety, confusion, or reduce pressure over misunderstandings, by observing body language and adjusting language as needed.*
- *Provide frequent encouragement and reassurance.*
- *Frequently check for understanding.*
- *Use concrete language and avoid abstractions.*
- *Break tasks into small chunks or steps.*
- *Show pictures or videos or model an action to get new information across. Often, the child is not able to translate verbal directive into concrete action. They need to visually see the action you wish them to do.*
- *Above all, be compassionate, empathetic, and patient with the child.*

# About the Author

G oretti E. Rerri was born and raised in Nigeria. She attended the University of Ibadan, Nigeria, where she obtained a bachelor's degree in English in 1979 and an MBA with a marketing concentration in 1985. In 2000 she earned a master's degree in education, specializing in special education, from Xavier University, Cincinnati, Ohio.

She is certified to teach special education from pre-k through high school in the state of Texas, and has been teaching in that capacity in the last seventeen years. Over the span of her career, she has taught students with various forms of disabilities, including autism, down syndrome, intellectual disability, cerebral palsy, ADHD, and learning disabilities.

She has worked as a classroom teacher, a parent trainer, and an In-Home trainer of students with developmental disabilities. Rerri has also mentored a number of new teachers in the field of special education.

An advocate for people with developmental disabilities, Rerri founded Emur Disability Advocacy Incorporated, a non-profit organization, whose flagship is the *Emur Awards*. The *Emur Awards* seeks, recognizes, and honors children and adults with developmental disabilities who have made meaningful contributions to their schools or communities. The awards are given in the month of March, each year, in celebration of Developmental Disabilities Awareness Month.

*My Box of Chocolates: How My Child with Autism Learned to Read, Write and More,* is her second book. Her first book, published in 2003, is titled, *Ceremonies and Festivals: Marriage, Burial, Chieftaincy, and Annual Festivals in Uvwie-Urhobo, Nigeria.*

Rerri has three grown children and lives in Houston, Texas, where she continues to work as a special education teacher.

# Resources

## Resources on Autism

1. Autism Speaks, Inc. Last modified 2017. https://www.autismspeaks.org.
2. Autism Society, Accessed March 30, 2017. http://www.autism-society.org.

## Resources on all Disabilities

1. National Institutes of Health. www.nih.gov.
2. Emur Awards, www.emurawards.org. Last modified 2017

## Resources on Disabilities in Your State

The ARC, Last modified 2017, www.thearc.org.

# End Notes

i. "History of Autism," *WebMD,* accessed March 30, 2015, http://www. webmd.com/brain/autism/history-of-autism.

ii. Benedict Carey, "Bernard Rimland, 78, Scientist Who Revised View of Autism, Dies," *New York Times,* November 28, 2006, accessed March 30, 2015, http://www.nytimes.com/2006/11/28/ obituaries/28rimland.html.

iii. Carey, "Bernard Rimland."

iv. "Autism Spectrum Disorder (ASD)," *Centers for Disease Control and Prevention,* accessed December 30, 2014, http://www.cdc.gov/ ncbddd/autism/index.html.

v. Margalit Fox, "O. Ivar Lovaas, Pioneer in Developing Therapies for Autism, Dies at 83," *New York Times,* August 22, 2010, accessed December 30, 2014, http://www.nytimes.com/2010/08/23/health/23lovaas. html?_r=1.

vi. "Building the Legacy: IDEA 2004," *US Department of Education,* accessed January 4, 2015, http://idea.ed.gov/.

vii. "History of Autism"

viii. Temple Grandin and Catherine Johnson, *Animals in Translation: Using the Mysteries of Autism to Decode Animal Behavior* (New York: Scribner, 2005), 19-26.

ix. Grandin and Johnson, *Animals in Translation,* 17.

x. Grandin and Johnson, *Animals in Translation,* 24.

xi. Lindsey Biel and Nancy Peske, *Raising A Sensory Smart Child*, August 2009, Sensory Smarts, accessed July 29, 2016, https://www.sensorysmarts.com/index.html

xii. Grandin and Johnson, *Animals in Translation*, 114.

CPSIA information can be obtained
at www.ICGtesting.com
Printed in the USA
LVHW04s2301140518
577225LV00001B/122/P